Here's a book which will help anyone in a leadership position in any organisation. Although it is heavily and obviously influenced by the author's Christian beliefs, and will therefore resonate with leaders of churches and church school communities - and a copy should be sent to all new Church School leaders by their Diocesan guardians - it will inspire leaders from other faiths and even those still searching, like me. Why? Well, it explores the vital issue of values and faith as the pre-requisites of leaders. And it does much more, with every chapter bringing into sharp focus some aspect of leadership, better enabling a leader to align what they say with what they do and with who they are.
Sir Tim Brighouse

This work is a collaborative invitation to organisational health, which is both thought and action-provoking. Sue presents many workable models for organisations to find clarity, focus, order and effectiveness. From diagnosing an organisation's macro issues, navigating through to the minutiae of each individual's motivation, she teases out important issues to examine. Theories and ideas are shared from her many years of valuable insight and experience. There are numerous tools to empower wise and godly paths, leading to the possibility of meaningful change.
Sue's narrative is a powerful testimony, sharing both the lens of her journey as it happened, later reflection on her work and how this was impacted from her relationship with God. She has articulated the essence of her life's calling and work, reflecting on her own golden threads. Whether you are leading a bank, school or church you will find this helpfully-coded book an encouraging and ideas-laden resource. If you are a member of an organisation, you will benefit from reading this book to inform your personal contribution to your organisation.
Alison Cansdale, Coach Mentor Supervisor Lecturer

We are living in a period of uncertainty and discontinuous change. The leadership stakes are high, with great opportunities alongside significant challenges. How do we navigate a way that will enable the organisations and communities we lead to flourish and fulfil their calling? Experienced educationalist, Sue Iqbal, has drawn on her experience and wide knowledge to bring together ancient wisdom and up-to-date research, offering an approach that is clear, practical and life-giving. A real strength of this book is that it does not champion one magic bullet but rather introduces the reader to a range of theories and applications that allow the leader to pick up and practice what resonates for them. The author writes simply and accessibly but don't be fooled; this is a book to read and re-read carefully if you want to enjoy its riches and lead authentically from within.
Paul Bendor-Samuel MRCGP, MBE. Executive Director, Oxford Centre for Mission Studies

Sue is driven by a restorative vision of highly effective Christian leaders in all sections of society who can root their purpose clearly in a deep understanding of their faith. **Golden Threads** *is therefore a timely and valuable addition to this vision, creating a rationale and toolkit to support experienced leaders, empower developing leaders and restore the passion and drive for those leaders for whom the past few years have been overwhelming. My prayer is that its readers learn to explore its depth and breadth of resources in a way that inspires them to create churches, communities, workspaces and organisations that enable people to realise their true potential and value.*
Neil Flint, Leadership Development Consultant and Coach

A thoughtful, provocative, well signposted, practical handbook for the Christian leader wanting to engage in the hard work of restoration and bringing hope. Her use of metaphors throughout the book is a powerful thread, which allows the reader the space for their own imagination to shape their meaning for their context. Though aimed at the Christian leader, this is definitely a book who's wisdom demands a wider audience.
Paul Duncan, Agape Europe VP Team

Sue has provided a fantastic resource for Christians in any sphere of leadership, whether it be church, school or elsewhere. This book is a mine of great ideas, models, principles and good practice and is written from her own substantial experience and observations. All leaders need help. Help has arrived in the form of **Golden threads.**
Nick Cuthbert, Founder, Lead Academy

Having worked alongside Sue for a number of years, I have found her to be an authentic, wise, purposeful and a highly relational leader.
The **Improving from WithIn** *model that Sue explains in this book works. It is not just theory it's a practical tool kit founded on biblical truths, drawing on practitioner perspectives and Sue's vast experience, knowledge and wisdom. It's full of gold that I wish I had read at the beginning of my leadership journey.*
Andy Worthington, Head of Church Relations Open Doors UK and Ireland

Sue Iqbal matches her wonderful, received wisdom with years of experience across senior leadership within both the education and the church sector. She has coached so many people in our community and has a beautiful blend of gentle challenge and directive insight, loving to facilitate healthy transformation.
As our chair of trustees, Sue steered us as a church leadership through significant change and transition, applying so much of the knowledge and best practice contained within this excellent book. It is very refreshing to gain insight and wisdom from someone who has dedicated so much of their time to walking with those in leadership. I highly recommend Sue's book and the wonderful model and best practice within it. If you are in leadership in any context this will be a blessing.
Judy Moore, Church leader and author

GOLDEN THREADS

Wisdom for authentic leadership and thriving organisations

SUE IQBAL

Copyright © Sue Iqbal, 2023

Published 2023 by Waverley Abbey Trust, Waverley Abbey House, Waverley Lane, Farnham, Surrey GU9 8EP, UK. Registered Charity No. 294387. Registered limited company No. 1990308.

The right of Sue Iqbal to be identified as the author of this work has been asserted by her in accordance with the Copyright, Designs and Patents Act 1988, sections 77 and 78.

All rights reserved. No part of this publication may be reproduced, stored in a retrieval system, or transmitted, in any form or by any means, electronic, mechanical, photocopying, recording or otherwise, without the prior permission in writing of Waverley Abbey Trust.

For a list of National Distributors, visit waverleyabbeytrust.org/distributors

Unless otherwise indicated, all Scripture references are from the Holy Bible, New International Version® Anglicised, NIV® Copyright © 1979, 1984, 2011 by Biblica, Inc.® Used by permission. All rights reserved worldwide.

Other versions used are marked: AMP Amplified Bible, Classic Edition (AMPC) Copyright © 1954, 1958, 1962, 1964, 1965, 1987 by The Lockman Foundation; ESV The Holy Bible, English Standard Version. ESV® Text Edition: 2016. Copyright © 2001 by Crossway Bibles.

Every effort has been made to ensure that this book contains the correct permissions and references, but if anything has been inadvertently overlooked, the Publisher will be pleased to make the necessary arrangements at the first opportunity. Please contact the Publisher directly.

Concept development and editing by Waverley Abbey Trust.

Design and layout by Simon Ray.

Printed in the UK

Print ISBN: 978-1-78951-451-3

Ebook ISBN: 978-1-78951-452-0

This book is dedicated to my husband Karamat who encouraged me to write it and our children, Hannah and Adam, who I trust will discover their own golden threads and maybe remember those we shared at the dinner table during our conversations and 'the best bit of the day'.

CONTENTS

Preface	9
Foreword	11
How to Use this Book	13

SECTION 1 – BACKGROUND

Chapter 1: Picking Up the Threads — 17
A brief biographical introduction to the author and the influences that brought her to faith and to the career choices that have informed her experiences and thinking.

Chapter 2: Drawing the Threads — 27
Explores the theories and experiences taken from a career in education and leadership and describes the process of drawing these threads together to create the model Improving from WithIn. The Improving from WithIn model is introduced and its six dimensions explained.

SECTION 2 – IMPROVING FROM WITHIN DIMENSIONS

PART 1: Building the Foundations – Chapters 3, 4 and 5

Chapter 3: Alignment — 41
Concepts of alignment and consistency are explored, and the relationship between core mission, vision, values and practice is explained. A case for alignment as a fundamental building block to organisational effectiveness is made. The chapter closes with the challenge for Christian leaders to align to biblical teaching.

Chapter 4: Climate Creation — 55
Climate, ethos and culture are explored and defined. Includes a five-step process to building a positive climate. A range of theories and tools from both secular and Christian literature, to guide leaders in creating climate, is presented. The chapter ends with a challenge to live out the fruits of the Spirit within organisations.

Chapter 5: Leading Change — 71
Leading change well is the challenge of every leader. This chapter provides helpful tools and theories selected from best-practice literature from a range of sources that have proved helpful throughout Sue's leadership work. We are reminded to lead with love and of God's agenda for change and transformation.

PART 2: Enabling and Nurturing Outcomes – Chapters 6, 7 and 8

Chapter 6: Innovation   85
The chapter starts by exploring the link between innovation and creativity and draws on positive psychology. It offers some practical ways leaders can nurture innovation, and gives a word of caution on how creativity can be stifled by leaders. Application in church leadership is offered, with an extract from Rick Warren's work. The chapter concludes with a call to use our creativity to further God's kingdom.

Chapter 7: Motivation   95
This chapter focuses on motivation, presenting key theoretical models and thinking and their application in organisations. It includes a range of actions leaders can take to increase the motivation in others. Christian teaching exploring the Dynamic Cycle of Grace is unpacked – with acceptance at the heart of the gospel, we can be released by motivation based on love.

Chapter 8: Engagement   107
This chapter explores the link between engagement and human flourishing, and draws on positive psychology theories. It offers a framework for discovering personal strengths and direction based on coaching work. The chapter ends with implications for church leaders.

SECTION 3 – COLLECTIVE WISDOM FROM CHRISTIANS IN LEADERSHIP

Chapter 9 : Interviews with Christians in Leadership   123
Based on interviews with fifteen Christian leaders from a range of sectors, this chapter explores what it is like to lead change in practice and how to navigate the complexities of leadership. Working in both secular and Christian contexts, these leaders seek to live out their call aligned to their faith.

SECTION 4 – FINDING GOLD

Chapter 10: A Call for Restoration: Letter to Today's Nehemiahs   145
What is the role Christian leaders can play in restoration following the pandemic? This chapter is aimed towards those tasked with restoring and improving a very broken and hurting world. Through metaphor taken from the Japanese art of Kintsugi, it urges leaders to rebuild with seams of gold and create something more beautiful.
The chapter offers some questions using the six dimensions from Improving from WithIn to help leaders respond to challenge ahead.

SECTION 5– DIAGNOSTIC CHECKLIST TOOL

Chapter 11: Diagnostic Checklist: Improving from WithIn   157

Appendix – McKinsey 7-s-based diagnostic tool   165
References   170

PREFACE

'What's bubbling up in you?' I often ask my coaching clients, and I urge them to be true to what they are sensing. This book is what has been bubbling up in me as I reflect on my working life, now with the space and time to articulate those reflections through writing. This is not just a retrospective project; it is also an attempt to weave the golden threads taken from sacred and secular wisdom to create a new tapestry which brings revelation to those who view it.

I am told that the strands of thinking, woven together into a new model, bring a fresh perspective where there is currently a gap in written material. I expect there are many conversations and works I don't know about, and my hope is that, in writing this book, others will respond by sharing these, so that together we can begin to fill that gap.

I began writing in February 2020 and throughout the next two years this book evolved. It has been shaped by my observations and experiences of the shared trauma of the COVID-19 pandemic and the human endeavour to adapt and respond to this global threat. I have observed the creativity and determination of the science community to discover vaccines and effective medical interventions. I have watched the resourcefulness of individuals and organisations working in new and previously unimagined ways. In spring 2022, I wondered how we would move forward and take those who were weary and finding hope elusive into a space where they could create a better future.

In the early weeks of the pandemic, I was self-isolating along with many others the world over. I reflected that Coronavirus had already transformed our lives and we lived in daily fear of what might still be to come. From my isolation, I wondered what life would be like and what truths we would need to guide us through the post-COVID-19 season. Command and control leadership had rightly risen to take charge of the crisis, but what next, as we were trying to rebuild on different foundations? Writing in April 2022, the pandemic was still rumbling on, more quietly and, in the predominantly vaccinated countries, without the level of fear it once had, but now we had new challenges ahead.

Maybe this work will help in these times, when new shoots have to grow through the desolate places; when we have lamented and grieved for what is lost. Leaders will work to restore what can be restored, rebuild with new tools, and maybe we will have learned some lessons about what is truly valuable, which can guide us forward.

I wonder who next will hear the call from God Nehemiah heard – the faithful prophet and leader from the Old Testament – and rebuild our walls. I pray for them to know that voice and lean into God, and for God to grow in them His vision and to give them the wisdom and strategy to bring it into fruition.

I am not an academic but by nature a practitioner who has applied theories and synthesised them to teach others in accessible language and simplicity. For those looking for academic writing, this work may not appeal, but for those open to complex concepts made simple, I trust it will satisfy.

I am fascinated by ideas and the application of theories and mental models and, over my career, I have gathered a rich toolkit of these; many are included in this text. I am also a storyteller and I have woven both styles together. Our learning styles are different, and most readers will know their preferred one. I hope that the blend of 'textbook' and narrative styles will appeal across the range.

Where I refer to a theory, model or research, I have endeavoured to identify its roots as I believe it is important to understand where ideas come from. I have also endeavoured to explain theories simply and to illustrate their application.

My aim is to reach people who are seeking ways to draw wisdom from the sacred and secular in order to guide the way they lead, grow and develop their organisations so that people thrive and flourish.

FOREWORD

Here is a book that is fresh in its approach and captivating in content. I read the draft at a time when at least two of the organisations I am associated with were coming to terms with the challenges of a new reality brought about by the pandemic. In Sue I found the guide I needed to help me look at the issues we were facing with fresh eyes. I am grateful.

Sue and I have shared a common history... not that we knew it. We first met when we were both serving in Church of England education work, mainly in schools. As we talked, I realised that there were probably many people like us – those who had become Christians early in life, had asked God for direction for our careers and had been led into teaching. At first, we thought that this was simply where our interest and capabilities had taken us, but then we came to realise, with some surprise, that this was a vocation, a God-given ministry to serve children and young people in the school context. Being connected to local churches, often with additional responsibilities there too, we began to see that there was much to learn about church life, its leadership, vision, relationships and culture... from the world of education. But also vice versa: we found much to take into school leadership from biblical models of church life. Sue and I, in our separate spheres, sought to think more deeply about these interchanges, learn from them and put them to use, both in the workplace and church. In this book, Sue's golden threads skilfully weave together a lifetime of wisdom, drawing on her wide experience in schools, with policymakers, local authorities and diocesan education teams. There is gold here.

Readers who work predominantly in education will find a distillation of so much that has been helpful in our field over the years, but with a fresh and powerful new approach in the shape of Sue's 'Improving from WithIn'. Her work on alignment, for example, is both compelling and challenging.

Others, who spend most of their time in church ministry, will find that Improving from WithIn will help draw out a perspective on church life that will be life-giving and help lead in exciting directions.

I have often reflected on the word 'interpreter' – someone who fully understands two languages, not just the words but the sense, and can effectively translate, enabling communication and understanding.

In Sue, we have someone who understands… no, I want to go further… *loves* the two spheres of education and church life: she has given much of her life to both. In this book our 'interpreter' opens windows that allow light to stream from one to the other, for the enrichment of all.

Rev Derek Holbird
February 2022

HOW TO USE THIS BOOK

This work has evolved during the writing process. In reaching Chapter 10 I realised that the book starts with the metaphor of golden threads and concludes with one of seams of gold; my aim to bring something precious to enrich leadership is the thread that runs throughout. To follow the thread, it may be helpful to read the narrative sequentially. However, the different sections provide opportunities to dip in.

This is both a textbook and a narrative, and I have provided the stories behind the theories and tools I have found helpful, and a rationale for using them. The lessons I have learned from my career in education, and then more widely in other leadership settings, I hope will be applicable to Christian leaders in a range of contexts. To aid the reader I have inserted the following icons to indicate Research, Theory, Mental Model, Process, Tool and Checklist.

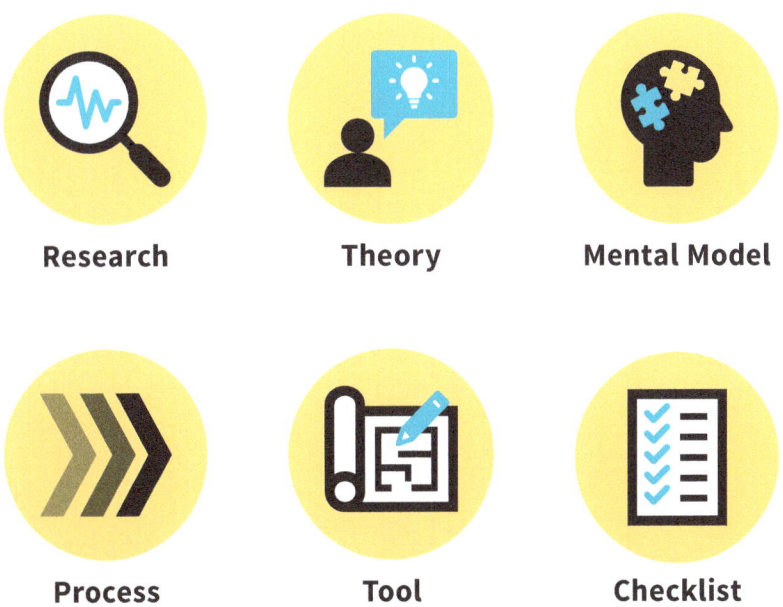

Research **Theory** **Mental Model**

Process **Tool** **Checklist**

In Section 2, Improving from WithIn is introduced and each of the following six chapters explores the individual dimensions. The model is designed to follow a process, with each dimension building on the previous one. The first three are the foundations that need to be in place to achieve the outcomes in the second half of the model. That said, readers wanting to explore individual dimension themes can dip into the relevant chapter. The chapter headings are colour coded to indicate which dimension of the model they explore.

Section 3, 'Collective Wisdom from Christians in Leadership', can be appreciated as a 'stand-alone' resource. However, there are references to the main text that provide the context.

Section 4, 'Finding Gold – A Call for Restoration', brings the reader back to the thread of gold and speaks to those tasked with leading us forward.

SECTION 1:
BACKGROUND

Chapter 1
PICKING UP THE THREADS

I was born into the baby-boomer generation. My childhood was unextraordinary. My father was the breadwinner and my mother relinquished her working life when I was born, only to pick it up again when I was 16, and then part-time. We lived in suburbia, south of Manchester, except for a couple of years in southern exile in Kent due to job relocation and then subsequent redundancy. Returning to south Manchester at the age of 9 enabled me to benefit from a grammar school education and to be the first in the family to attend university.

My experience growing into teenage years was that of freedom, gathering with friends in the local park or at their homes, riding my bike to visit the library, Friday tea at my grandmother's and visiting my godparents in the Cheshire countryside at the weekend. I was a Brownie and then a Girl Guide. I attended Sunday school because it was a prerequisite to joining the Baden-Powell movement. I said the Brownie Guide Promise; in those days it required me 'to do my duty to God'. I read my prayers from a Ladybird book of *The Lord's Prayer.* At school I sang hymns in assembly and, each Christmas, was treated to a candlelight carol service with full choir, which was the only time of year when my parents attended church.

When I was 13, something happened that made an imprint on me and for which I will be, literally, eternally grateful. The gang of friends who gathered in the local park and sat on the benches behind the tennis courts included a group of slightly older boys. Their exploration of teenage freedom included rock music, alcohol and smoking what they referred to as 'dope'. The ringleader of this group was charismatic, modelled himself on Roger Daltrey from the rock group, The Who, and played his guitar very loudly, often with bedroom windows open to enable the whole street to enjoy it.

In March 1973, this aspirational rock star had a Damascus Road experience, discovering Jesus and the Holy Spirit through the ministry of a local Pentecostal church. One of the first things he did was talk about his experience of being reborn and becoming a Christian. One evening my friend and I were together at her house – she lived over the road from him – and he came and explained what had happened. I remember going home feeling extremely uncomfortable and perplexed. I thought I was a Christian by virtue of being white, British, middle class and attending Sunday school. Why did I have to 'become' one? Was this true? And if I did, how would I know, and would it make any difference?

This discomfort continued. It took me a few weeks to find the answers to my questions and required several conversations with older members of church youth groups I'd joined. On 22 March 1973, I decided to invite Jesus into my life and to become a Christian. I cannot remember exactly how I resolved my queries, but I can recall a genuine spiritual experience of lightness, excitement and peace.

In 1973 there was a widespread movement of revival amongst young people, initially from the Jesus People in the USA and moving throughout the UK. It was the summer of *Lonesome Stone*,[1] the musical by the Jesus People. This melded together the San Francisco hippy conversion story with rock music, and captivated my peers. There were also initiatives called 'Call to the North' and 'Come Together', which seemed to galvanise and legitimise the movement. As a response, my local parish church opened its doors to an ever-growing youth group on a Friday night; that and surfing other such groups facilitated my early discipleship journey.

On rediscovering my first-ever Bible from those early days, I saw written out in capital letters a verse from the book of James: 'be ye doers of the word, and not hearers only, deceiving your own selves' (James 1:22, KJV). I remember that call to authenticity becoming an incredibly significant thread for me. It touched a value of integrity deep within that I was unaware of at the time but which has since become one that guides my life. Many years later, I recall looking around at the friends I had invited to join me on my 40th birthday, thinking, 'What quality distinguishes these people?' and concluding, 'Integrity'.

One of the other benefits of my discipleship journey in the mid-1970s was access to other young people and adults who were also processing their theological thinking. I attended regular Bible study groups, some of which were intergenerational, and I learned to express my thoughts and realised my ideas and opinions were valued. These experiences were foundational in developing self-confidence and encouraging me to not be overawed by others.

At school I was an unremarkable student, progressing satisfactorily through O levels, now GCSEs. In my sixth form I was given the opportunity to do community service and I chose to work in a special school on Wednesday afternoons. It was here that my first introduction to teaching began, and the appreciation of the power of reframing an idea to help a child learn a concept was cemented. I can remember to this day helping a boy who had spina bifida with his maths. I asked a question and could see that he just did not get it. Intuitively I was prompted to ask the question in a different way, and I saw a lightbulb go on and his joy, then, in understanding. The impact of this on me was transformative. I knew I wanted to teach, and I was drawn to working with children who had additional needs.

My journey into teaching in the late seventies was through undertaking a specialist Bachelor of Education degree. Having three years to delve into education studies, philosophy, sociology and psychology, as well as specific learning theories for children with special needs, was a rich experience. At the end of my second year, I had the opportunity to work in an adult community for people with learning difficulties in upstate New York. I was fascinated to see the application of theories such as behaviour modification in action, and again appreciated the power a teacher who understood psychology, motivational and learning theories could wield.

When I graduated, I began working with adults who had learning difficulties. As a first job, it was exciting to be tasked with creating a curriculum to enable these adults to gain greater independence. I realised that I thoroughly enjoyed the creativity of designing learning activities and materials. After a couple of years, I made the transition from working with adults to working with older children in a school setting. In my third and most significant teaching job, I was appointed to develop the 16 plus provision in a special school. The school catered for children from 2 to 19 years; some of my students had been at the school for 14 years by the time they arrived in the Further Education Department. Creating a climate that was distinctly different and afforded them adult status was my aim. This in turn placed an expectation on them to behave in new ways and I was surprised to see the impact this had on raised motivation and their learning. Understanding that my behaviour and that of my colleagues enabled a climate to be established that was significantly different for the students was a powerful lesson.

The school I worked at was highly successful and had some extremely dedicated teachers and classroom assistants. I began to appreciate the impact of strong leadership and the way an organisation perpetuates its ethos to secure a climate by articulating its values and expectations. Here I could see the need for all to 'walk the talk' and how that integrity provided the psychological safe environment for encouraging professional development and commitment, and generated a generosity of spirit to go the extra mile.

Teaching these young adults as they endeavoured to gain the skills to become more independent inevitably required helping them navigate sex and relationships. In the early 1980s there was little recognition that this need existed, with some parents still being told their children would never reach sexual maturity. Having worked first with adults and now with older teenagers, I had begun to develop curriculum and materials to address this need. As a result, I unexpectedly became an expert in the Birmingham Special School community. This took my career in a new direction and opened opportunities in the field of health education and advisory work.

In 1990 I made a career move away from school into an advisory role, which had the added attraction of being part-time and allowing me more time with my own children.

I cannot underestimate the significance of this move in developing my thinking and in the subsequent opportunities it presented. These enabled me to establish myself both regionally and nationally. I taught and facilitated teachers developing Personal Social Health and Moral Education, wrote guidelines for schools, ran projects, and spoke on behalf of the city of Birmingham. Throughout this, I continued to learn more about how human beings thrive, learn, change behaviour and lead effectively.

As a Christian, working in the field of Health and Sex Education presented some challenges. There were competing forces at work; it was not always easy to discern which policy direction to support or recommend. I was increasingly placed in positions of responsibility, often being asked to speak on behalf of the Local Authority. This was frequently with the press and occasionally in response to lobbying groups of politicians. I recall being summoned to the House of Lords to meet with a Christian lady peer who, knowing I was a fellow Christian, expected me to have undue influence on the policy for the city. I remember being asked directly, 'What is Birmingham's view?' and genuinely thinking, 'I haven't got a clue – it depends on who you ask!' I was aware of her views but also of the complexity of navigating the diversity of viewpoints and communities we served in Birmingham.

I was conscious that my job was taking me into situations that required greater wisdom than I possessed and that few of my friends had such experiences. I felt a little exposed and unsupported but felt that my situation was far from unique. I began to develop links with the Christian Charity CARE, who had an interest in education, and was fortunate to gain a partial secondment to support the development of the network, Christians in Education. The aim was to provide a safe space for Christian leaders to meet and discuss ethical dilemmas.

My personal journey had deepened my understanding of the importance of values. In 1980 in my final year at university, I had met my future husband and, despite much opposition to our relationship due to his Pakistani background, we married in 1983. On a visit to Pakistan in 1986 to meet his parents, I realised that our family values were remarkably similar and that those had become the foundation for us to navigate difference.

In 1995, working on sensitive issues and across Birmingham (which was, even then, one of the most diverse cities in the UK), I came to realise the power of values to unite or divide. I began to work on values in education and subsequently I led the Birmingham Values for Learning Project under the sponsorship of our Chief Education Officer, Professor Sir Tim Brighouse.

In 1996 the education debate in England had started to consider what the curriculum for spiritual, moral and social education should be. In response, the School Curriculum and Assessment Authority invited educationalists to contribute to a National Forum. The aim was to gain consensus on, and provide schools with, a statement of shared values. There was an emerging political struggle, backed by the strengthening Labour Party, to promote citizenship education and a tension between secular and religious ideologies. The Archbishop of Canterbury concluded in a speech in April 1997 to the Values and Curriculum Conference at the Institute of Education that these shared values were an important starting point, and they should be promoted in English schools whoever won the General Election.

The privilege of being involved in the School Curriculum and Assessment Authority (later Qualification and Curriculum Authority) working group meant that I experienced philosophically deep discussions with very well-informed and erudite people. During this time, my conviction grew about the significance of values in schools. I could see the link between these values and the practical outworking of them in creating an ethos or school climate. Creating a secure psychological environment was critical to a school's success, both for its pupils and for the staff serving them. I experienced schools where the staff all 'walked the talk' and those where they did not, and the impact in the latter was often a climate of insecurity and in some cases toxicity.

The Birmingham Values for Learning project culminated in a conference in September 1997, with keynote speeches from professors Ted Wragg and Marianne Talbot and representation from the then Department for Employment and Education. This conference gave Birmingham school leaders the opportunity to join the national debate and apply it to the Birmingham context. Through the King's Fund we funded a small number of schools to engage across the generations in 'Intergenerational Dialogue' about values in their communities. Discussing what is really important was surprisingly easy and the agonies of the national debate seemed insignificant faced with the pragmatism and realism of school communities.

In 2001, a colleague and I wrote *Benchmarks for School Ethos* as part of the Success for Everyone[2] series published by the Local Education Authority. This work provided school leaders with a framework to build a secure ethos as well as a toolkit for how to approach it. I worked with individual schools to help them explore the interplay between values, school mission, vision and practice. Articulating these complex interrelationships and exploring the value of integrity enacted as 'walking the talk', I became aware of how an organisation builds consistency by aligning practice with its values.

Personally, these experiences were very significant. I had begun my transition from health education consultant to a school leadership advisor, and this was further facilitated by the emergence of the National College for School Leadership, which was one of the flagship projects the Tony Blair government instigated as a response to their 'Education Education Education' mandate.

By 2004, I had found myself at the National College being trained to deliver leadership programmes. This suite of programmes drew heavily on the theories previously seen in business leadership and management books, much of which came from the disciplines of business leadership and management or organisational development. The Hay Group were involved in making these theories accessible to an educational audience. One of the best ways to learn is to teach. Facilitating other adults to learn about these theories and apply them to their school leadership embedded these concepts in my own thinking. I found myself drawn to those stemming from positive psychology and coaching.

Parallel to my formal career I was training in the art and skills of coaching. I undertook a Diploma in Performance Coaching and began seeing individuals who needed help in discerning direction or a career change.

The schools advisory service had two main functions: overseeing the educational standards of the city's schools and developing and equipping its workforce to provide education effectively. The challenge to see all schools providing quality education was measured by pupil outcomes, and schools that were considered to have perpetually underperformed were prescribed school improvement remedies. The tone of the national discussion was becoming more hostile and such schools were now frequently referred to as 'failing' schools.

My involvement in this was part of the National Challenge Programme as a facilitator on 'Developing Your Senior Leadership Team'. I remember vividly one weekend event, with a team voluntarily participating in a residential being threatened by a senior colleague – should they not turn their school around, there would be consequences. This experience and others during the latter part of the 2000s began to make me feel uneasy. Teachers were being prescribed not only a national curriculum but how to teach. Lesson observations with expectations of a prescribed pedagogy were the norm, and gradually the autonomy and creativity of teachers were being eroded. The culture of anxiety was increasing, and teachers and school leaders were losing professional confidence.

By 2011, austerity had begun to impact on education services and I took voluntary redundancy. Now working for the Forward Partnership, a company my husband and I had created in 2000, I was free to work more widely across the region and on a variety of projects. One of the fruits of this was to take some space to reflect on the tension between target-driven cultures and human motivation. I came upon the book *Drive* by Dan Pink[3] and suddenly things crystallised for me. The increasing use of the stick rather than the carrot was killing creativity and motivation in schools; there must be a better way of achieving improvement – harnessing human motivation that enabled pupils and staff to thrive.

Sir Ken Robinson gave a TED talk on 'Do Schools Kill Creativity?',[4] firmly concluding there was a danger that they did. Against this backdrop and reflecting on many conversations with like-minded educationalists, I began to sense something bubbling up in me.

One day in 2012, I sat down at the breakfast table and drafted out a model for values-based school climate improvement, which I called 'Improving from WithIn'. This process wove together the strands of positive-psychology, values-driven improvement and was underpinned by a biblical view of human flourishing. I felt in the creation of the model that I had begun to articulate wisdom drawn from both secular and sacred traditions. The title of the model deliberately gives emphasis to intrinsic motivation by spelling 'WithIn' with a capital 'I'. Intrinsic motivation, the pull towards something as a motivator, reflects both a rubric from positive psychology and the invitational nature of God's call to follow Jesus.

Working in the predominantly secular field of education had often challenged my personal faith position. I navigated it with care, especially when I was the lead officer for sex education and as teenage pregnancy coordinator in 1999. I was conscious that being a person of faith evoked suspicion from certain individuals. I found it particularly challenging to balance my role with my beliefs. That said, my overwhelming experience has been that truth stands and that wisdom is not the domain of a one-belief system. I came to notice the people who reflected light and truth, together with those opportunities to capitalise on and take initiatives that were, in essence, good. The golden threads catch the light and illuminate even the darkest picture.

In 2013 I had the privilege of working for Coventry Church of England Diocese, which was setting up a new Multi-Academy Trust. This role enabled me to influence the underlying philosophy for school improvement as the Trust was established. It also gave me the opportunity to consider the theological strands in more depth. I will be forever grateful for this experience.

I left full-time working in July 2017 and am now back working flexibly for our company. I divide my time between Christian leadership and life coaching, consultancy work, designing and delivering courses on leadership, and coaching. I have finally had the time to gain accreditation as a senior practitioner coach with the European Mentoring and Coaching Council. In December 2019 I attended an EMCC symposium during which I sat in a group with Professor David Clutterbuck and engaged in a conversation about organisational improvement.

Occasionally I have felt a specific call to action: once, which led to the birth of Improving from WithIn, and secondly during this discussion. What was being talked about were concepts I had included in my model. I resolved to write my book so these could be shared more widely.

In this chapter I have endeavoured to explain how I have gathered the two golden threads during my life that have finally come together in the model of Improving from WithIn. As life happens, we often don't notice how one thing leads to another, but incrementally we grow and deepen our understanding. As these two threads have been woven into my tapestry, the picture they have formed is full of light and texture. I hope to share it with you in the rest of this book.

Chapter 2
DRAWING THE THREADS

In 2011 I took voluntary redundancy from the local authority; had I not, within a few more months, redundancy would have happened anyway. By choosing to leave, I gained a little bit of control over the timing. Over the years I had watched older colleagues retire from service, with the obligatory retirement 'do' and kind words offered in praise of their service to education in Birmingham, and that is what I had always expected would happen to me too. So, my leaving a rapidly reducing advisory team, who no longer met to wave each other off, felt sad and an anti-climax after 30 years of teaching and advising in a city I'd been proud to contribute to.

Now working as an independent consultant for our company, I was naturally concerned about earning an income. This was a season for trusting that God would provide. I believe He did. I was truly fortunate to pick up some substantial consultancy work, which took me into schools across the West Midlands region. This broadened my perspective further and enabled me to understand the variety of contexts across the area. I worked in Stoke-on-Trent, Telford, Worcestershire, the Black Country, Warwickshire and Coventry. The work I was involved in was the creating and delivering of bespoke leadership development and, significantly, with senior leadership teams.

My work included using a diagnostic process based on the McKinsey 7-S[5] framework for organisational effectiveness. This tool had been developed by a small team of consultants working out of HTI (Heads Teachers and Industry). We were passionate about the need to get under the skin of an organisation before designing or delivering any intervention. The members of the original core team were some of the most creative, generous and effective leadership consultants I have ever worked with. We worked collaboratively on the diagnostic and subsequent offer to schools, but by far the best aspect of our times together were our sharing of a tool or technique, thus developing our own repertoire of skills further. I learned so much from this group and will be forever grateful for this opportunity.

As I worked with senior leaders and their teams, I appreciated the impact of leadership style in creating the climate for schools to improve. I became convinced that really effective leaders were able to bring about an alignment between the school context, their vision for the school, the school values and actual practice, which included processes and systems that enabled the vision to be realised. In the pressurised world of school improvement, and for schools that were 'failing', an unrelenting focus on teaching and learning was the building block for success. Often, though, the heroic leader sent in to rescue a school was unable to shift their style once the crisis had passed, and capacity building was required. Teachers were given a prescription for how to improve but in that process, some were losing their professional self-confidence and doubted their own judgments. I could see that although improvements to teaching were enabling students to learn, the climate in the school often became one of dependency on the leader. A feature of the conversations I was having with both teachers and their leaders was a loss of motivation and confidence.

As the education landscape embraced the concept of System Leadership, the National College leadership programmes were being rolled out through teaching schools and many of the facilitators were existing school leaders. Some were brilliant and offered chalk-face immediacy as well as the craft of developing adult learners. Some, however, were not as adept, and the raft of expertise gained by years of lead facilitators specialising in effective adult learning was being diminished.

By 2012, this work had begun to dry up and I had more time to reflect. It became a season of sabbatical, and as I began to synthesise my thoughts and consider the prevailing climate for schools, I sensed I was birthing an idea but at the time did not know what it was.

This chapter is about drawing the threads together from my experiences in the education sector, the connections I made as ideas crystallised, and how I birthed my model, Improving from WithIn. As a believer in the 'spiral curriculum' (in favour in the 1990s), in which each experience as a learner builds on previous ones, for me the formation of my ideas and the specific threads of thinking grew out of my experiences. It is helpful to look back to the early years of my teaching career, as they shaped me.

When I consider my early teaching experience, I was fortunate to work at a time when the National Curriculum was not prescribed and, for the special school sector, was absent. Creating a curriculum for the newly formed Further Education Unit was a formative and learning time. In researching best practice, I visited other schools and talked to more experienced teachers. One of the benefits of looking at others' practice was to consider what would transfer to our context, analyse what was good practice and distil from that how we might approach and develop our curriculum.

We spent endless hours discussing the reasons behind the curriculum and pedagogical decisions we'd made. The two years spent working with the deputy headteacher to create 'Towards Independence', a curriculum and assessment system to meet the needs of the students, was the best bit of Continuing Professional Development I ever did. I didn't resent the Sunday night meetings at her house, nor the trial and error approach to working out what was best. I took risks, got things wrong and tried something else. This very experienced teacher asked me what I thought and together we worked in what I felt was an equal partnership of discovery. She gave me the space to develop; I grew in confidence and my teaching skills evolved.

I remember recently, when schools were given freedom to choose their own assessment systems, so many young teachers felt adrift; the skills to design and own a system had atrophied in the teaching profession. I was someone who thrived on creating and having the autonomy to find my own way to solve problems. I had been fortunate to learn my craft as a young teacher in the 1980s.

In the early 2000s, with the introduction of the National College 'Leading from the Middle', 'Leadership Pathways' and mandatory 'National Professional Qualification for Headship', coaching began to gain popularity as an approach to developing leaders. The interest in using coaching in education and in school improvement grew. There was a curious conflict that also emerged – the tension between carrot and stick. Coaching worked best when people had capacity and time to consider their solutions. In sports coaching, practising specific skills over and over and using video feedback to increase self-awareness effectively improved performance. This was being translated into the classroom, and classroom observation with video and subsequent feedback developed.

The accelerating drive to improve pupil outcomes as a measure of the effectiveness of the school was gathering momentum, and school improvement, pedagogy and the curriculum were increasingly becoming more prescriptive. Estelle Morris, looking back on her time as Secretary of State for Education, remarked in a *Guardian* article, November 2014,[6] that she regretted the degree of government intervention and prescription for teaching and learning. She said, 'I failed to persuade my own party, but I still believe politicians should not tell teachers how to teach.'

One example that illustrates this tension comes from an experience I had co-delivering coaching training to a group of teachers in March 2011. We were working with teachers gathered from different schools for a two-day training event, developing coaching skills. By lunchtime on the second day, my co-facilitator and I were very satisfied with the way things were going; the group had gelled, the activities were well received and there was enthusiasm for using coaching skills. So, we started to discuss going back into the school setting and implementing these newly developed skills in the workplace. Something tangibly shifted; the more we discussed the reality of school, the less convinced the group members became that they could actually use coaching in their place of work.

My co-facilitator and I were so perturbed by this shift that we met for a day to reflect on what we had experienced. After much deliberating, we concluded that the climate in many schools was just not conducive to developing a coaching culture, and although coaching was effective in building capacity and developing teachers' skills and confidence, which schools aspire to do, the prescriptive and target-driven culture that was defining school improvement was making risk-taking, experimentation and coaching less realistic. Where coaching was being used, it might be to teach specific teaching skills at the more directive end of the coaching continuum.

In the previous chapter I have already described the impact of this on motivation for a group undertaking development through National Challenge. Another instance that impacted me greatly was as a consultant working with a team of faculty leaders in a secondary school, given the task of securing a uniform approach to teaching and learning across a school. It became evident that the team was divided between those who thought prescribing a framework for lessons was going to be effective and those who had, up until this initiative, always secured good pupil outcomes from a more flexible approach. One very experienced and effective teacher was at her wits' end. Having had a very successful career, she was considering throwing in the towel because she could not live with the level of prescription that was going against everything she held dear, and the wisdom gained from her cumulative years of experience.

If these illustrations are indicative of the climate facing teachers around 2011, it is little wonder that risk-taking, appreciative enquiry, peer-coaching and engaging in the type of curriculum and pedagogy development that enlightened my early career were rarer than they should be.

Schools do not function in isolation, they reflect the prevailing ideas of the times. I had friends working in many other sectors also struggling with the growing target-driven culture. A brief internet search will bring up a plethora of articles, such as this one from December 2016 in *Cambridge Independent*:[7]

> Writing for the *British Journal of Psychiatry*, Anglia Ruskin University Professor Jamie Hacker Hughes has called for the NHS to address the 'huge increase in staff sickness rates' that he says is due to the NHS's target-driven environment, requiring tighter and tighter performance targets.

In January 2012 Ofsted released a new framework for school inspections.[8] Within this framework was the drive to see pupil engagement as a measure of a good lesson. I remember tuning in to a broadcast explaining the changes in the framework and pondering how this was to be measured. It also occurred to me that, for many teachers, churning out engaging lessons day after day, against a backdrop of prescription of pedagogy and curriculum, was a big ask. The creativity required to engage learners also needed a degree of autonomy in how best to achieve this, as well as some much-needed respect for the professionalism of teachers.

Through my reading and online researching, I was becoming increasingly uncomfortable. There seemed to me to be a body of evidence and research that was being ignored by the educational establishment. I had previously discovered Dan Pink's book on motivation, *Drive*; I was watching TED talks by Sir Ken Robinson on 'Do Schools Kill Creativity?'. Whole Education[9] was founded in 2010 and a range of other thought leaders were all concerned at the reductionist view of education being touted by Michael Gove as the then Secretary of State for Education. Such voices seemed to be drowned out in the public arena as curriculum reform took place. The drive for school improvement was gaining momentum as the beginning of the move to force academisation onto 'failing schools' was increasing the pressure on the school sector.

My own view of education as a means of developing the God-given gifts and talents every child is born with, as well as giving the skills necessary for making sense of life, was very secure. I had seen children struggling with a particular subject, yet coming alive in others. Reducing the curriculum was something I felt was going to disproportionately disadvantage the less well-off and those whose parents did not augment education with sport, music and arts activities. I was sad to see the initiatives, such as Children's Centres and Extended Schools Programmes championed by the Blair Social Exclusion Unit, being abandoned.

Working with adult learners had changed my view of pedagogy too. I could see the increasing opportunities for facilitating learning and welcomed ideas such as the Flipped Lesson.[10] Much of this debate was undertaken in the educational intelligentsia, or 'The Blob' as Michael Gove named it. Sadly, power rested elsewhere, and education has endured many more years of fluctuating thinking on releasing of prescription on pedagogy and focus on the breadth of curriculum.

Back in early 2012, my mind was absorbed by the concepts and ideas arising from the world of positive psychology about human flourishing, the biblical view of Christ coming to give 'life in all its fullness' (John 10:10, NCV), the concept of Shalom, and the lessons I had learned about how organisations thrive and become more effective. I was conscious of the mismatch between these ideas and the prevailing mechanistic view of school improvement. I concluded that if those ideas were true, there must be a better way to release intrinsic motivation to secure improvement through developing a climate for thriving.

As an educationalist, I was aware there was an ever-increasing resource telling headteachers what to do to improve their school; an army of consultants willing to provide advice and, in some cases, write plans and policies for busy school leaders. I wondered if there was too much out there; were we getting lost in the depth and breadth and complexity of it? Or was it possible to draw together the strands of wisdom from existing practice and thinking and produce a simple model that combined these strands into a logical format? I concluded that it should be. I was seeking to do just that: present a logical model, which was flexible enough to tailor to different contexts but contained key dimensions and an underpinning philosophy to guide the leader.

Improving from WithIn came about from considering the 2012 OFSTED framework and the challenge of producing learning experiences that are both motivating and engaging, and during which progress is made. What support did teachers need to do that consistently, and how should leaders invest in developing that same motivation and engagement for the teachers? I believed that teachers who are motivated and engaged are far more likely to be able to motivate and engage their pupils. For this to happen, school leaders needed to create the climate which enabled this to occur.

When writing *Benchmarks for School Ethos* in 2001, I had begun to understand the power of the 'air we breathe' in an organisation and to articulate what the component parts were in creating it. Working with school leaders on leadership style and grasping the incremental impact of specific leadership behaviours in promoting, or sadly, in some cases, negating a set of values, had reinforced my view that climate could be designed. Effective leaders were intentional in doing this. They were self-aware and strategic about developing the atmosphere to enable the vision for their school to be realised.

The next fundamental consideration relates to what we know and believe about how adults learn and improve their performance. Here, there are two key theorists who have shaped my thinking. First is Richard Boyatzis with his work on Intentional Change Theory.[11] Boyatzis argues that for adults to make change that is sustained, they need to be motivated, and that motivation is created by a pull towards an ideal. His model provides a series of discoveries that support the individual in achieving change.

The second is Daniel Pink. In his book *Drive*, Pink argues that when you take basic human needs out of the equation, there are three key drivers that motivate us: autonomy, mastery and purpose. These motivators are intrinsic and more effective than extrinsic ones, such as money or negative forces, or the threat of punishment.

These theories, along with the wisdom gleaned from the discipline of coaching and the emerging field of positive psychology, demand that we reconsider how we lead and create the conditions for school improvement. School improvement cannot be 'done to' but needs to harness the energy of intrinsic motivation within its community and be driven by its members. Leaders need to create the climate within which motivation and engagement are likely outcomes for the adults as well as the children.

In response to this, Improving from WithIn was born. What would school improvement look like if it were influenced by understanding how humans thrive? What should 'life in all its fullness' (John 10:10, NCV) feel like inside a school? How do you release intrinsic motivation and inform good practice in adult learning or change theory, such as Richard Boyatzis' 'self-directed change' model? What might the outcomes for pupils be if the teachers really owned the enactment of curriculum, and were themselves fully engaged in honing their craft and ensuring the experiences they created for their pupils were compelling? What would be required of leadership in creating the climate to make this possible, and how would this learning community articulate its values to a wider audience?

One morning in early 2012, I sat at the kitchen table and literally, on a piece of paper, began to draft out a model for a values-based, positive approach to creating the climate for school improvement. My questions had been, 'If these things I believe in are true, what would it look like? Where would you start?'

Transferability to Other Sectors

Throughout these introductory chapters, I have drawn from my experiences in the education sector, and the model I will present was originally designed for the school sector. However, as with other theories that are derived from the researcher's specific focus but have wider application, I believe that my work has wisdom for other organisations and have used it within Church and Christian Charities to inform work on core mission, vision, and leadership practices.

Drawing the Threads

THE IMPROVING FROM WITHIN MODEL

Improving from WithIn © 2012 Sue Iqbal. Forward Partnership

Six Dimensions

Alignment
This is the process of alignment between the core mission (or purpose) of an organisation – its vision, the values it promotes – and actual practice.

Climate Creation
The climate is secured by unrelenting attention to secure consistent behaviours that promote the underpinning beliefs and agreed values; these behaviours become 'the way we do things around here' and, when adopted by the whole community, create a secure ethos.

Leading Change
Leading change requires effective leadership behaviours, strategies and skills; it also requires an understanding of positive psychology and an appreciation of human flourishing and motivation to ensure that all adopt new behaviours and are empowered and take ownership of change.

Improvement and Innovation
Improvement, when truly effective, arises out of a desire to make things better, to solve problems or to master new skills. It is a creative process which needs to be owned by the members of an organisation. It's often a cycle that requires experimentation, trial and error, revision and refining. At its best, this creative process will invite innovation.

Motivation
In order for human beings to thrive and to perform at their best, they need to be motivated. Extrinsic (external) drivers are far less motivating than intrinsic(from within a person) ones. Organisations able to harness and encourage intrinsic motivation will outperform the rest.

Engagement
When human beings are motivated, they become engaged; when they are engaged, deep learning and high performance take place. In such organisations a climate of meaningful purpose develops, along with behaviours associated with 'going the extra mile' and generosity of spirit.

Two Sides of the Model

Foundation Stones
Alignment, Climate Creation and Leading Change are the foundations which need to be in place to enable the outcomes of self-sustaining improvement to be achieved.

Outcomes
Innovation, Motivation and Engagement are the outcomes of an established, aligned, self-sustaining improvement culture.

THE MODEL DIMENSIONS

The model is comprised of six dimensions. It is designed to be used incrementally, with the concepts relating to each dimension helping to build a climate for engagement. Organisations will have different starting points as some aspects of their practice will be established whilst others are not.

Later in this book, I will give some diagnostic questions to help leaders pinpoint where to begin their focus. In the next six chapters, I aim to introduce each dimension in more depth, to give a rationale for their inclusion and the theories, both sacred and secular, that underpin them.

SECTION 2:
IMPROVING FROM WITHIN DIMENSIONS

Part 1: Building the Foundations

Chapter 3
ALIGNMENT

Key Concepts: Core Mission, Values, Vision and Practice

I have observed that achieving alignment and consistency is the fundamental task of a leader. Deciding on what to align to, though, is the critical starting point. I believe there are some significant building blocks that can assist leaders in this task. The foundation stone must be an articulation of why the organisation exists, its core purpose or what its *core mission* is. This sounds simple but requires the leader to consider some deep questions. What are we about? Why do we exist? Why are we distinctive? What would be missing if we didn't exist?

For some settings it may appear to be quite simple: a school is an educational establishment, or a church is a body of Christians – however, it is important that a school community or a specific church can articulate why they exist and what they stand for. Understanding the community they serve, their specific needs and what strengths they offer can inform this process further. One of my sadnesses in observing school mission statements in recent years has been the number that have regurgitated OFSTED-pleasing phrases or the approved 'British Values', rather than offering a distinctive articulation of why that school exists and what it seeks to do.

In some Christian-based organisations that have grown from an initial 'call' or vision, I have observed there can be a drift from the founding purpose because of changing circumstances or funding arrangements. Is there a case for revisiting the founding purpose and examining what still stands in the current context? Do organisations need to re-articulate or be recommissioned for a new purpose in a new season?

The problem facing organisations without a clear core mission is that, in the vacuum, others will build a narrative. The powerful voices in staff teams can create an alternative narrative that meets their needs or reflects their beliefs and, because of their perceived power, they often gain willing followers. This can cause confusion or undermine the ability of a leader to move the organisation forward. Sometimes the leader is the problem: there is a leadership vacuum because the leader is pulled in many directions or doesn't have a clear sense of what their organisation is for. This is where the Trustee Board, directors or governors will need to step in and secure the core mission, and make courageous decisions about how best to support the current leaders or secure more robust future leadership.

The next step is to express the *values* of the organisation: what does it stand for? What behaviours does it expect, and what can others expect to see outworked in practice? This link between what the organisation says it stands for and the actual practice people observe indicates how embedded those values are. Where they are not, the gap between what we say and what we do can become a seed bed for cynicism, which can lead to demotivation and division.

When working on the Values for Learning project I noticed that many schools had 'respect' as a value. I would ask, 'What does *respect* look like on a wet Friday afternoon as you walk down a busy corridor?' This reality check is helpful because where there is little evidence of respect, the next question might be: 'So, what should we be seeing down that corridor and what can we do to make sure that is what we experience?'

Values are an expression of what the organisation believes in or what is important; they inform how work will be conducted and the priorities set. They are a guideline for how people should behave and how they can expect others to behave. When embedded in an organisation, they create a psychological safe space within which a certain set of behaviours occurs.

Values come from our deeply held beliefs; they are shaped by our experiences and by how we get our needs met. We all have them; they will guide how we behave. For many of us, they are subconscious, but we become aware of them when we are asked to behave in a way that conflicts with them. In an organisation, with many individuals, all with their own values, gaining alignment to a specific set of values is vital to ensure the organisation can achieve its core mission and that everyone is pulling in the same direction.

The Iceberg Model

The *Iceberg Model*[12] is often used to show that most of what influences behaviour goes on under the surface. Edward T. Hall devised the model to explain the dimensions of culture.

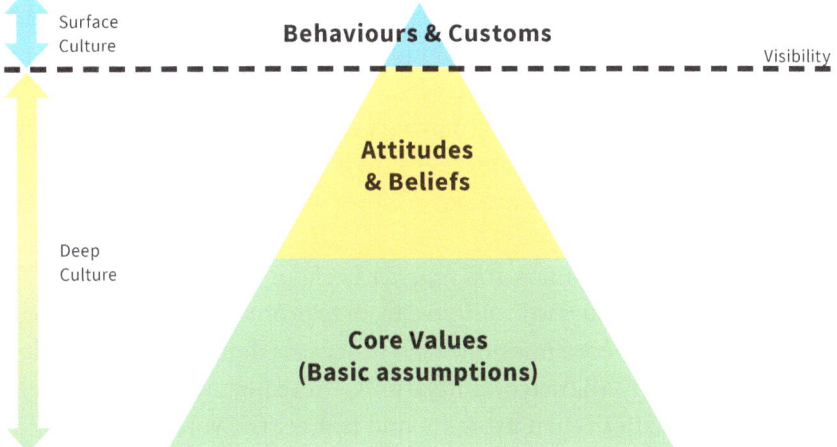

Adapted from *Beyond Culture*. Edward T. Hall 1976

What we see and experience is the visible outworking of values, a set of behaviours and customs that define an organisation. What is unseen are the attitudes, beliefs and core values that underpin these.

It is clear from this model that leaders will need to invest in conversations that address attitudes and beliefs and be explicit about what the core values of their organisation are. The journey to align individual values to those of the organisation is one which requires great leadership skills and intentional behaviours. The leaders need to continually promote these values and ensure that behaviours and practices are consistent.

One of my observations as a young teacher was of an effective headteacher. He frequently focused on a specific aspect of practice that needed aligning. It would appear casual, but his actions were intentional. He would wander into the staff room just before the end of lunch break – this had the effect of all staff returning promptly to classrooms prior to the start of lessons. Respect for the students' right to well-prepared learning environments was strengthened and expectations made clear. Another example would be the leader who always noticed specific contributions of individual members of the team. An email or note would appear to thank them. In this case, for a leader who publicly declared that he valued individuals, this example of 'walking the talk' built loyalty, respect and a culture where going the extra mile became the norm.

I have also experienced situations where the stated values of an organisation are constantly undermined by leadership behaviours that negate those values. Here the gap between what is said and what is actually done is glaringly obvious. The impact is loss of respect for the leader, division and dissent, lack of moral purpose and an inability for the organisation to progress. The psychological contract is broken and members do not feel safe in such situations. The 'rules' they were meant to follow are not adhered to and the outcome is often workplace stress.

The link between values and *practice* is clear. I have made a case for practice and behaviours to be aligned to, or to promote the organisational values to serve the core mission. This process is demanding for leaders but in successfully aligned organisations, these behaviours are 'caught' by others who will in turn promote and protect the values.

The final building block in this dimension is *vision*. Where is this organisation going in the future? What does it aspire to do? How is it responding to challenges or an expected future? All organisations need to have a compelling vision from which the strategic direction is set, and out of that, specific action plans are devised.

With a clear view of the core mission, explicit values, expected behaviours and practices, the organisation needs to create a vision which is compelling. People are drawn to vision; they will have an emotional response to it. A desired future is attractive and people will follow it. Richard Boyatzis describes the power of the 'Positive Emotional Attractor'[13] in his work on intentional change. A vision becomes compelling when it describes an ideal future that is better than the status quo, so the risk of not achieving it becomes unattractive and people will invest in making the vision a reality.

In the absence of vision, people have no sense of direction and will respond in different ways: some will fill the void with their own narrative; some will hunker down and keep the status quo; some will disengage and lose motivation. Personality, level of experience and seniority will all impact on these responses – what is clear is that the organisation is not effectively harnessing the collective potential.

I have worked with many leadership teams and individuals on creating vision and have seen the power a compelling vision can have in releasing a desire to make a preferred future a reality. The pull towards it energises and inspires.

I have been involved with leadership teams who invest time in co-creating vision, often in response to a particular set of circumstances or external change. Those who have a clear view of their core purpose (mission) and understand their values base have the foundation of a shared language with which they can engage in imagining what a future might look like.

Once created, achieving an organisational vision is complex and will require leaders to manage change effectively. Leading Change is the third dimension of the model, which I will come to in Chapter 5.

When I worked on Values for Learning, I began to understand the interplay between mission, vision, values and practice. To help others understand this I created a mental model to illustrate it, which I called the Plumb Line Model.[14]

GOLDEN THREADS

ALIGNMENT: INTERPLAY BETWEEN MISSION/PURPOSE, VISION, VALUES AND PRACTICE

 **The Plumb Line Model**

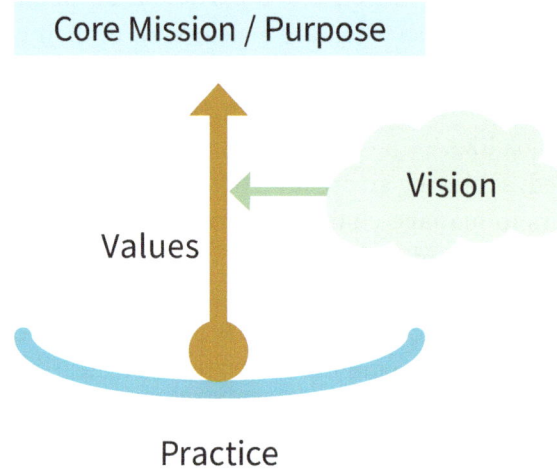

The Plumb Line Model ©2017 Sue Iqbal. *Updated from Values for Learning 1996*

The core mission or purpose once agreed stays the same; it is the enduring reason for an organisation to exist.

The vision is the strategic direction of travel for a given season to enable the core mission or purpose to be achieved.

The values are the enduring qualities and ways of being adopted by the organisation to ensure behaviours stay true and exhibit the qualities that are expected within it.

Practice is what actually happens and what people do or say.

The role of the leaders is to identify and secure a vision that will move the organisation forward, keeping practice true to the mission/purpose and the values in order to execute that vision to best effect.

If practice and behaviours are not aligned to the values, the trajectory will not stay true to the mission, and the core mission and vision will not be achieved. This is illustrated below.

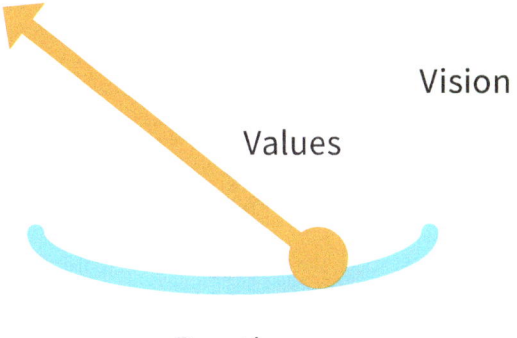

ALIGNMENT IN ORGANISATIONAL EFFECTIVENESS

Models and Using Diagnostics

Much has been written on the importance of alignment in organisational development and effectiveness. The two examples I have included here are ones which particularly resonate with me.

I mentioned working with the McKinsey 7S Model. This is a powerful tool to illustrate the complexity of an organisation and how the various elements interrelate with each other, developed by business consultants Robert H. Waterman Jr and Tom Peters in the 1980s.[15] They argue that, for an organisation to perform well, the seven elements (being structure, strategy, systems, skills, style, staff and shared values) need to be aligned and mutually reinforcing.

Working with this model and using it as a basis for a diagnostic tool for schools, I found it was possible to understand the strengths and weaknesses of an organisation and see where different aspects needed to be realigned. Breaking down the complexities of an organisation into these seven elements enabled leaders to see where they needed to focus their efforts.

The McKinsey 7S Model and Theory
Adapted from 'McKinsey 7S' by Sue Iqbal 2010

Thinking Strategically	Is about the way in which we look ahead and create a vision of where we need to be in the future, and how we communicate this to others in order to achieve high-level buy-in.
Establishing Structure	Is about establishing the way things are structured in order to deliver the vision. It is about clarity of roles, responsibilities and lines of accountability.
Designing Systems	Is about the way in which we create effective mechanisms in order to get things done. It implies effective communication, transparent, clear decision-making, and implementation of actions.
Building Capacity (Skills)	Is about organisational learning in order to achieve improvement, change and sustainability.
Creating Climate (Shared Values)	Is about creating conditions in which people work effectively together in order to achieve shared goals.
Developing Leadership (Style)	Is about the behaviours and qualities of the people who leverage change so that they influence others through a range of styles and skills.
Maximising Human Resources (Staff)	Is about ensuring that all staff have the capacity, competence and commitment to fulfil their role.

In an abstract published in the *Journal of Educational Administration* in 2007 by Christopher M. Branson[16] entitled, 'Achieving Organisational Change Through Values Alignment', Branson argues that 'widespread resistance to organisational change is caused by a failure of current organisational strategies to attend to a values alignment process for all those people affected by the desired change'. He continues, 'this paper proposes that values alignment may not just be an important integral part of organisational change strategies; it could well be the bedrock, the foundation, on which all truly successful organisational change depends.'

These theories echo my experience of working with leaders who aim to change and improve their organisation. Those who are successful address all the complex elements in their organisations; they do not neglect those elements that are unseen or below the waterline in the Iceberg Model.

SACRED PERSPECTIVES ON ALIGNMENT

Aligning to God's purpose and His teaching is a recurrent theme throughout the Bible. There are many texts and stories that illustrate this. The image of a plumb line is used in Amos, chapter 7, to illustrate a measure of justice and truth which Israel was judged to be forsaking. This image teaches us to align to God's teaching and indicates that we are often unwilling to do so. It is no surprise that the image is particularly significant to me having used it for my own mental model.

Recalling my early Christian life in the previous chapter, I mentioned having written out the teaching of the apostle James:

> Do not merely listen to the word, and so deceive yourselves. Do what it says. Anyone who listens to the word but does not do what it says is like someone who looks at his face in a mirror and, after looking at himself, goes away and immediately forgets what he looks like. But whoever looks intently into the perfect law that gives freedom and continues in it – not forgetting what they have heard but doing it – they will be blessed in what they do. (James 1:22)

Alignment to God's purposes means obedience to, and acting on, His Word.

During a visit to Coventry Cathedral in 2013, I came upon the beautiful sculpture, 'The Plumb Line and the City'[17] by Clark Fitzgerald, depicting a city with the plumb line of judgment hanging above it. Personally, this has huge significance as it speaks to my values of integrity and alignment, and is a wonderful artistic interpretation of those values. Coventry was devastated during the Second World War and the old cathedral was ruined. In its place, the new cathedral and a new city emerged. The builder's plumb line, or God's judgment, reminds the viewer of the need to keep true to that line in the rebuilding.

The Plumb Line and the City by Clark Fitzgerald. Photo by Jim Linwood, Flickr

In the Book of Proverbs, aligning to and seeking wisdom is given as advice for living a prudent life, the fear of the Lord being the source of all knowledge. Obedience to God's teaching and applying it to your life will make you truly wise: 'Commit to the LORD whatever you do, and he will establish your plans. The LORD works out everything to its proper end – even the wicked for a day of disaster' (Prov. 16:3–4); 'Trust in the LORD with all your heart and lean not on your own understanding; in all your ways submit to him, and he will make your paths straight' (Prov. 3:5–6).

There is a pattern in the Book of Proverbs in the way the individual proverbs are constructed – a contrast between the fruit of following God's way and a warning of not doing so. Whilst these verses can be taken out of context by those wanting to find God's blessing for their own plans, they provide a clear principle that to live well is to align to God's ways and seek His plans for our lives.

The Psalms, often a heart cry or prayer, plead: 'Show me your ways, LORD, teach me your paths' (Ps. 25:4), or 'Search me, God, and know my heart; test me and know my anxious thoughts. See if there is any offensive way in me, and lead me in the way everlasting' (Ps. 139:23–24).

The prayers of the psalmist declare that he wants God to show him how to live life and find direction towards His ways: 'Who, then, are those who fear the LORD? He will instruct them in the ways they should choose' (Ps. 25:12); 'I have considered my ways and have turned my steps to your statutes' (Ps. 119:59); 'Your word is a lamp for my feet, a light on my path' (Ps. 119:105).

One year I decided I would read and meditate on a Psalm each day. The experience taught me how to pray, and of the rawness of the human condition as the psalmists poured out their emotions to God. I also noticed that, however raw those emotions were and whatever the dire circumstances, the writers ended by praising God or surrendering to His will. I love the authenticity of the Psalms and the way they indicate that to align to God's will or to follow His way is not always easy and is no guarantee of a painless life.

In the New Testament, much of Jesus' teaching through stories and parables presented a challenge to received wisdom of the day. It called for His followers to live differently, aligned not to the religious law but to God's Kingdom. In the Lord's Prayer, Jesus taught us to pray, 'your kingdom come, your will be done' (Matt. 6:10).

A feature of God's Kingdom is love: Jesus commands His followers to love one another. This is reiterated by Paul in his teaching on love to the Corinthian Church.

My own belief is that, as humans, we were designed to thrive best when following our Maker's instructions, applying these in our organisations by aligning His 'kingdom values', expressed as the fruit of the Holy Spirit. This is the plumb line for shalom.

ALIGNING YOUR HEAD, HEART AND GUT WITH GOD

I attended a retreat in April 2019 during which I learned how important it is to align our head, heart and gut – or, more simply, our thoughts, feelings and intuitive sense. I learned to separate out my focus so I could tune in to my cognitive processes, emotional and intuitive brains. Three-brain theory is well researched but is something I hadn't fully appreciated until this retreat.

The retreat was for successful leaders, many of whom were adept at articulating their thoughts but had lost the connection with their emotions or intuitive selves. The facilitators skilfully probed and encouraged us to explore our deeper feelings and intuitive senses.

As we did, a new understanding of ourselves emerged and we were all better able to make life decisions and positive changes for the future.

Talking with Alison Cansdale, fellow Christian coach, I have discovered that she includes a fourth element – head, heart, gut, *God* – which enables the person to consider, 'What is godly teaching in this?' or, 'What might God be saying?' is even more helpful.

Using the 'Head, Heart, Gut, God' Tool

Often, we don't feel at ease with decisions or a situation. This can be because we are experiencing an internal struggle to align our thoughts, feelings, intuition and what we understand to be biblical teaching, or what we sense God is saying. When these are not all aligned, 'shalom' will be elusive. However, when they do align, we have a deep peace and hope which enables us to make decisions or to accept a situation.

I now use this approach in my coaching and will ask clients to go through a process exploring each 'brain' in turn, giving time to hear what God may be saying. We then work with anything that comes up that seems misaligned. For example, a client who wanted to move forward as a leader sensed a call from God to do so and was capable and skilled, but emotionally couldn't imagine herself leading others due to feelings of inadequacy. As we saw where the main area of blockage came from, she was able to confront her feelings, identify where they had originated and challenge herself to see her future differently.

I offer this simple tool to help you explore this approach further.

Alignment

Coaching Tool: Working with Head, Heart, Gut, God

HEAD
- Place your hand on your head
- What are you thinking?

HEART
- Place your hand on your heart
- What are you feeling?

GUT
- Place your hand on your stomach
- What are you sensing?

GOD
- Place your open hands out in front of you
- What are you receiving from God?

Chapter 4
CLIMATE CREATION

Key Concepts: Ethos, Climate, Culture

The second dimension of the Improving from WithIn model is Climate Creation. This is another of the foundations that needs to be established to enable the organisation to flourish. An organisational climate is complex. It is comprised of multiple layers that include behaviours, customs, ideas and beliefs, and ways of being. As a concept, it is difficult to define and the language used is often interchangeable: character, ethos, spirit, culture and climate. A climate is felt and observed rather than decreed. It may be far removed from the stated narrative of leadership.

I will use the following terminology as these words are in use in the organisations I am most familiar with: climate, ethos and culture. I offer below the definitions of all three from the Cambridge Dictionary.

> **Ethos:** the set of beliefs, ideas, etc. about the behaviour and relationships of a person or group.
> **Climate:** the general development of a situation, or the situation, feelings, and opinions that exist at a particular time.
> **Culture:** the way of life, especially the general customs and beliefs, of a particular group of people at a particular time.

It is clear from reading these definitions that they do overlap and, in certain settings, some are more frequently used than others. Schools are used to the concept of 'school ethos' and other organisations will describe their 'culture'. We can see from the definitions that ethos arises from a set of beliefs, culture is formed from customs and beliefs, and climate describes how it feels at a given point in time.

I also note that both climate and culture include 'at a particular time'. This is helpful because it means they are not set in stone and if they are able to change with time, something must happen to make that change.

In 'Benchmarks for School Ethos' (2001), I defined ethos as 'a unique school culture that is based on a set of shared values and which is developed and promoted through consistent practice throughout all aspects of school life'. My observation from working with leaders from all organisations is that ethos, climate and culture are concepts that seem intangible. As such, leaders often find it difficult to articulate what they mean and consequently to make changes that impact positively on them.

What helps in making these concepts tangible is to clarify the component parts and focus on them. These parts comprise a set of beliefs or values, specific behaviours, feelings and opinions, customs, and ways of conducting relationships. Wise leaders will ask questions to identify how it really 'feels' out there: what behaviours are the norm? Are the customs they have promoting or negating their values?

In Improving from WithIn, the Climate Creation dimension is about understanding the aspects of organisational life that contribute to creating a climate for thriving. In understanding those aspects and imagining what might provide the catalyst for change or impact most on culture, the leader can begin to build a climate that serves their core mission, and preserves and promotes the positive values they seek to embed.

Boyatzis' Theory of Intentional Change: Model and Process

WORKING WITH CLIMATE 5-STEP PROCESS

In working with leaders and their teams, I have discovered that following a process can be helpful, and I offer a 5-step process for you to consider in building your climate. One of the influences for this process is **Boyatzis' self-directed change model** (see fig. 1 – note that fig. 2 applies the model to organisational change). In his model, Boyatzis identifies key discoveries that help to create a positive motivation or 'pull' towards making a sustainable change.

The 5 discoveries are:
1. The ideal self and creating a personal vision
2. The real self and gaining a view of current strengths and weaknesses
3. A learning agenda or plan for change
4. Experimenting with new behaviours thoughts and feelings and practicing those
5. Identifying trusting relationships to support the process of change.

Fig 1

Richard Boyatzis, Model for Intentional Change 2000[15]

Fig 2

Intentional change theory at the organizational level: a case study:
Van Oosten: Journal of Management Development. Vol. 25 No. 7[19]

Climate Creation Process

Step 1: Establishing the Baseline

One of the most energising times in my career was when I was appointed as a Deputy Diocesan Director of Education for Coventry Diocese, covering the areas of Warwickshire, Solihull and Coventry, each with its own Local Authority and with differing approaches. My first task was to get under the skin of this new area; to understand the context, identify the challenges and grasp the prevailing climate. This focus on diagnostic work is a fundamental step any new leader has to undertake in order to establish their starting point. New leaders inherit a climate and need to understand it, identify the aspects that are positive and those which are not, and then decide which to change.

For established leaders there can be a challenge in viewing their organisational culture with fresh eyes. This is because 'this is just the way we do things around here' has become familiar. Some find it difficult to know where to start and how to notice and challenge accepted norms. In working with established leaders, I have found that using staff feedback questionnaires or interviews can provide valuable insights and help to identify 'blind spots' that may have been overlooked.

Establishing the baseline is about getting a clear view of the current reality: what is really going on? Is what we say we are about actually happening in practice? This is the 'real self' or second discovery in Boyatzis' model. The first discovery in his model is to identify the 'ideal self'. In my experience, the ideal or preferred future may grow from understanding the current reality and context.

Step 2: Gap Analysis

The second step arises from the work in the Alignment dimension of the model. Leaders need to consider the gap between what they have discovered about their organisation's climate baseline and the elements of core mission, values and vision. Is what they are seeing or hearing moving their core mission forward? Are the collective behaviours promoting the values? Is there a compelling vision that inspires followership, not only of tasks but also of behaviours?

This **gap analysis** is critical in identifying what needs to be addressed. Leaders should be asking themselves, 'If that is what I want it to be like and this is what it is actually like, what can I change and where do I start?' The imagined vision of the future gives leaders an appreciation of what it will look like, how people will feel and what they will say and do. By describing the vision as a set of tangible behaviours, the leader can attend to making those behaviours a reality.

Step 3: Leadership Behaviours

I believe the most powerful tools the leader has in creating the climate is a control over his/her own leadership behaviours. By modelling specific behaviours, leaders can have an impact on how people feel and what they experience. Climate is created by an unrelenting attention to leadership behaviours. Which behaviours does the leader need to model in order to see the change they envision? This is the third discovery in Boyatzis' theory, described as the 'learning agenda'.

Working with one of the headteachers in the Values for Learning Project, I observed this process closely. An experienced but newly appointed head had begun to work in a large primary school, which was best described as chaotic. This visionary and quietly determined leader decided to take a values-led approach to school improvement. She discerned that the quality the school and the local community most needed was calm, so she set about modelling calm in every interaction. There was also a need to demonstrate that the school valued its children, staff and community. One example of this, which was appreciated by the staff, was flowers being placed in their refurbished toilets. The head shared her vision, gaining widespread 'buy-in' from staff and parents alike, and slowly the school became a calm and peaceful, purposeful place for learning.

In this process, I observed her intentionally **modelling the leadership behaviours** she wanted to see across the school community. This slowly established new behavioural norms. Children and staff were challenged when they exhibited negative or negating behaviours. In time, others took on the job of preserving and protecting the values by challenging each other.

Boyatzis refers to this stage as 'experimenting and practising'. As practice continues, new neural pathways become established. That is exactly what was happening in the case of this school's experience: the collective neural pathway was being strengthened by modelling, reminding, and reinforcing preferred behaviours. In time, these become established practice.

One aspect that is vital to protecting an established, positive climate is how new initiatives are implemented. The leader needs to consider how to shape them to their specific context and to ensure that they can be implemented in a way that preserves the existing climate. In the education field, where so much change is externally imposed, I observed strong leaders who did just that: they questioned, 'How can I implement this in a way that works well for our organisation and that will continue to uphold those things that are non-negotiable?'

Step 4: Engaging Others

In his model, Boyatzis suggests the identification of trusted relationships to provide support through the change process. No leader can change the climate on their own – they need to win over others to take on the task of behavioural change. Often a leader can identify those willing followers, or 'early adopters' as Everett Rogers calls them in his Diffusion of Innovations theory,[20] who will quickly take up new ideas and change their practice. Leaders can then work through these people to continue to embed behavioural change. In any organisation there will be a range of responses to change, and the next chapter will examine this in more detail.

The mark of the depth of an embedded culture is how many members of the organisation adhere to the 'preferred behaviours' so that these become the norm. I believe that healthy cultures are created by voluntary adherence to a set of behavioural norms. In unhealthy cultures it is possible to observe strong behavioural norms that are established by fear and reliant on compliance. These compliant behaviours are more likely to arise from external motivators and as such are less sustainable than those that come from intrinsic or internal motivators. Once the external pressure is removed, compliance will often cease, whereas well-established behaviours that are aligned to a person's intrinsic motivators and value systems will continue even when 'nobody is watching'.

Step 5: Enduring Legacy

Is it possible to so deeply embed a culture that the climate endures beyond the term of individual leaders? Here I return to the plumb line and the elements of alignment. If a core mission is clear, the values explicit and the practice aligned to these, I believe that, just as vision may be for a season, an organisation can appoint leaders for a specific season or purpose. In some cases, a change in leadership is needed in order to achieve the vision. The recruitment process will need to acknowledge the importance of values alignment and the role style of leadership and competence will play in maintaining and enhancing the climate. The

Hay Group work on organisational climate which builds on the work of Professor David McClelland's[21] four-circle model for effective leaders and organisations is a helpful resource to explain the interrelationships of these elements in creating an organisational climate.

In one school, at different times, I worked under three different headteachers and somehow the ethos (or school culture) didn't change. We used to observe new staff members arriving and it became obvious who would stay and who just wasn't aligned to the school's behavioural norms. In a timespan of seven years, somehow the culture endured. Established customs were perpetuated, behavioural norms and expectations were stated and the values were made explicit. During this time, we experienced a season when the climate was threatened by the sudden departure of a headteacher and, for a while, it felt insecure. However, the culture remained constant. The school weathered that storm because, even during it, the cultural norms were preserved and protected by a group of staff who were fully invested in seeking the continuation of the school's success. I learned much from this experience and concluded that cultural legacy can endure past an individual leader when shared by a team of committed people.

Using Models Flexibly

As with any model it is important to use it flexibly. This may mean starting at a different point or revisiting aspects as new information becomes available. I have used Boyatzis' model flexibly as a coaching tool. Similarly, those familiar with Sir John Whitmore's GROW model[22] for coaching may move between Goal, Reality, Options and Will multiple times in a coaching process.

GOLDEN THREADS

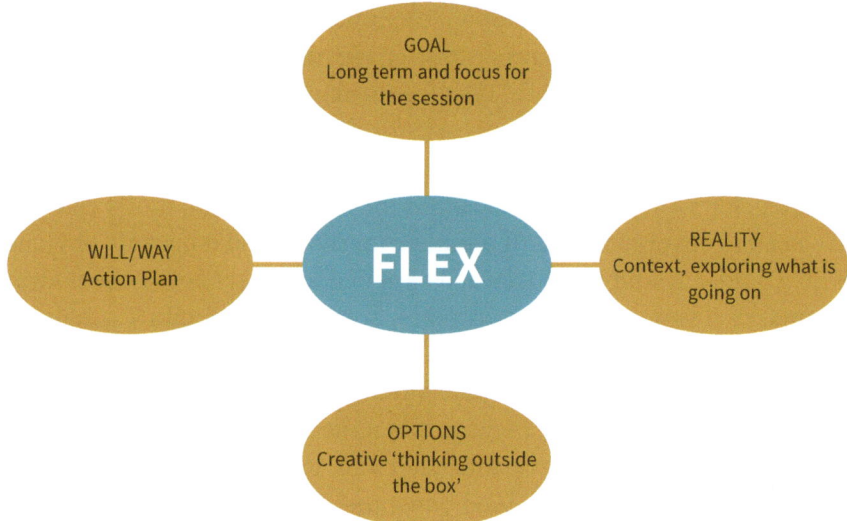

Sir John Whitmore's GROW Model

CLIMATE CREATION: RESEARCH THEORIES AND MODELS

Patrick Lencioni

There is a body of research that sees a link between organisational success and the climate within the organisation. One accessible publication is Patrick Lencioni's book, *The Advantage*.[23] In it, Lencioni makes a case that 'Organisational Health will one day surpass all other disciplines in business as the greatest opportunity for improvement and competitive advantage'. Lencioni draws on his 20 years' experience of writing, field research and executive consulting to present the Four Disciplines model.

Climate Creation

Discipline 1 includes five behaviours that need to be cohesive: building trust, mastering conflict, achieving commitment, embracing accountability, focusing on results.

Discipline 2 is all about alignment and includes key questions: Why do we exist? How do we behave? What do we do? How will we succeed? What is most important right now? Who must do what?

Discipline 3 is about regularly communicating the narrative of the first two disciplines so that people are reminded of them.

Discipline 4 is about creating structures and human systems that reinforce and bring the narrative to life.

I find many of Lencioni's observations on 'Organisational Health' resonate with me, in particular by making the component parts explicit and by describing the specific contributions of behaviours to building and maintaining a healthy organisational culture.

Application in Schools

 ### Matt Bawden's Checklist for Schools

For those working in schools there is much written on school ethos. Making the link between ethos and outcomes for students is important. Identifying the contribution school ethos or climate makes to student success brings ethos to the attention of school leaders and demonstrates the need for intentional leadership focus to ensure this is what it does. A recent article by Matt Bawden (Assistant Headteacher at Queen Elizabeth's Grammar School in Ashbourne and Editor of the Association for Character Education eJournal *Character Matters*), in SecEd January 2019[24], presents an argument for the power of school ethos in raising aspirations in students.

He writes:

> When considering your ethos as a living breathing thing, is it possible to see it at work in the school, helping to create a sense of drive and purpose for all concerned, or does it lie hidden in the policies and documents? Bringing it to life can have real impact on the success of the school, and in driving aspirations for all.

Bawden goes on to present three principles for making this happen. He describes the collective effort required to positively change the ethos to bring about desired outcomes:
1. The ethos is owned by everyone.
2. The ethos lives because we acknowledge it in our lives.
3. The ethos matters because we make it matter.

He continues with some practical ways to begin:
- Ask a range of people (students, staff, parents, local shop owners) what they think the school stands for, making sure those who may have struggled to be included are a part of this initial stage. Then compare the responses with what is on the website.
- Use some of these people to discuss what the ethos ought to be in relation to happiness and future success. An ethos ought to raise our aspirations – and not just for the few.
- Rewrite the ethos, vision and values statements in the light of these discussions, making everyone aware you have done it.

- Publicise the revised ethos, looking for every opportunity to show how it is a key part of daily school life (in lessons, in the extra-curricular, at lunch and in the community).
- When something happens that doesn't fit the new inclusive ethos, say so. Make it the reason for the punishment, the change to the curriculum plan, the introduction of a new club.
- When something happens that shows the ethos working for all, celebrate it. Sometimes people need examples to spur them on.

BUILDING CHURCH CULTURE

Samuel R. Chand's Checklist for Building Church Culture

Samuel R. Chand

Church leaders looking for specific models and literature for their sector may find Samuel R. Chand's book, *Cracking Your Church's Culture Code: Seven Keys to Unleashing Vision and Inspiration*[25] helpful.

Chand makes the case that, without an enabling church culture and systems, strategy will fail. He suggests leaders spend as much time working on creating a positive culture as they do on casting vision. He also offers the following seven keys of culture:

Control
Team members need to see themselves as partners in a grand venture. Good leaders involve everyone in the planning process. They give authority to match responsibility. Good leaders give clear direction, provide resources, and maintain accountability.

Understanding
Each person on a team needs to be clear on the way the team functions. They also need to be aware of each team member's vision, gifts, contributions, experiences, and heart.

Leadership
Organizations need to focus on the heart and character of people as they develop them as leaders. Healthy organizations are pipelines of leadership development.

Trust
Mutual trust among team members is the glue that makes everything possible. Trust takes time to build. It requires people who are honest, open, and transparent.

Unafraid
People face difficulties and challenges with courage if, and only if, they are convinced that what they are doing counts for all eternity and they believe in the people serving on their team. Great leaders welcome dissenting opinions, as long as people offer them in good will and with an eye toward a solution.

Responsive
For teams to be responsive, they must develop a consistent process for collaboration. Being responsive requires both a sensitive spirit and workable system to make sure threats and opportunities don't fall through the cracks.

Execution
System-wide failure to execute decisions poisons the atmosphere of an organization. To ensure that execution becomes the norm, you must clearly define goals, delegate well, measure progress, and hold one another accountable.

Getting Buy-in
Successful culture change requires buy-in from each person. Everyone on the team must become a willing partner in the venture.

Will Mancini

 Will Mancini's Process and Core Practices
In his book, *Church Unique*[26], Will Mancini offers a similar set of practices. He asks, 'What if we were to make even more conscious our intentions towards culture-shaping leadership? What core practices would come to the surface?'

The seven practices comprise:
1 Articulation: The first step of culture-shaping is to identify, name and define. That's what it means to be human- bringing meaning through how we label and distinguish within the created world and within the world we want to create. You can't mould in the real world what you don't hold in the mental world. So, what are you holding? What are your top three or four culture-shaping aspirations?

2 Imitation: You teach what you know, but you reproduce what you are. Your life is broadcasting and multiplying a values set. How is that values set being consciously transferred by you, even though the receiver may not know it?

3 Mechanism: If you lead a team or an organization, you have the authority to create a shared experience or a roll-out of a new process. Think of a mechanism as an event or process that clarifies, restores, aligns, or attunes your people with an existing shared value. Think of this as a wake-up call that shakes up business as usual.

4 Collision: Oftentimes values get clear and concrete at the very moment they are violated. Or it may be a time of testing or crisis that brings a "near violation." Look for collisions in the past and potential ones in the future to rehearse and strengthen values. As a leader don't be afraid to name when you missed a values-based decision or needed a realignment yourself. That may be the most important impression you ever leave.

5 Decision: Consciously run your decisions, big and small, through the filter or your values. Most importantly combine this with "imitation" and walk through a conscious decision-making process with your team using your values. What decisions are you facing today? What are your biggest decisions in 2012?

6 Question: Dialogue is one of the leader's greatest tools. And dialogue works best with questions, not answers. Ask questions to clarify, to meddle, and to rethink. Pose questions for your team to answer. Specifically bring bold questions that force new thinking around the same values.

7 Celebration: The most often cited culture-shaping activity is celebration. People repeat what's rewarded. Make sure you take time for this. If this is one of your perpetual weaknesses, assign someone on the team to plan the moments that mark your church's progress. Life is too short not to celebrate! Shape culture in churches.

These two church-based tools are similar to those suggested by Bawden for schools (see page 64). It is my belief that leaders from different disciplines and sectors have much to learn from each other and would greatly benefit from opportunities to share their collective wisdom.

SACRED PERSPECTIVES ON CLIMATE AND CULTURE

When considering the biblical influences on my thinking about how climate is created, I am drawn to St Paul's teaching on the fruit of the spirit. In Galatians, he writes about life by the Spirit:

> You, my brothers and sisters, were called to be free. But do not use your freedom to indulge the flesh; rather, serve one another humbly in love. For the entire law is fulfilled in keeping this one command: 'Love your neighbour as yourself.' If you bite and devour each other, watch out or you will be destroyed by each other (Gal. 5:13–15).

Here, Paul warns of the toxicity of not living lives driven by love. However, if we live by the Spirit, we will demonstrate the fruit of the Spirit: 'But the fruit of the Spirit is love, joy, peace, forbearance, kindness, goodness, faithfulness, gentleness and self-control' (Gal. 5:22–23).

These qualities, or fruit, are observed and experienced in the behaviours of those who live by the Spirit. When a group of people choose to allow their character to be made more like Christ and to live in step with the Spirit – collectively in a church community or an organisation – this will be experienced as a set of behavioural norms that reflect these fruits. This in turn will create a climate that is defined by the greatest commandment: to love one another.

Chapter 5
LEADING CHANGE

Key Concepts: Emotions, Motivations, Values, Beliefs

Leading Change is the third dimension of the Improving from WithIn Model. Leading change well is the foundation to building a flourishing, thriving organisation. I have outlined the need for alignment of core mission, values, vision and practice and, in the previous chapter, I described how leaders can impact on and create a positive climate. Now it's important to look at how leaders make change happen.

Leading and managing change is a subject addressed extensively in academic study, leadership journals, books, and by management schools and consultants. In my own research, development and experience, I have discovered and created models, tools and techniques that are helpful in supporting leaders to work effectively in change. Improving from WithIn is about changing organisations so that they thrive and the people within them flourish. In this chapter, I will outline the aspects of leading change that leaders must be aware of in order to do this well.

For organisations to change, leaders will need to identify what change is required. It is often tempting to focus on structures and systems as the key to change, and sometimes these do need to be looked at. However, if the leader is seeking the transformational change that will enable flourishing, changes that bring about new behavioural norms are needed. That is only possible if leaders are able to recognise that real change happens in the domain of emotions, motivations, values and beliefs.

The leadership toolkit required for this change is demanding because it necessitates leaders working on the below-the-waterline elements of the Iceberg Model. For this, leaders need to understand how people change and how they, as leaders, can create the conditions to help people change. They also need to have the level of self-awareness and emotional intelligence that enables them to reflect on the impact of their leadership style and their own behaviours.

I draw again on Boyatzis' model here: the ideal self translated to a thriving organisation in which its people and those they reach flourish. Working through the model, if that is the ideal, how do leaders go about establishing the 'real self'? For this they need to be honest and seek an accurate view of the current situation. Developing diagnostic skills is one such tool for this.

EFFECTIVE DIAGNOSTIC SKILLS

Leaders need to acquire the ability to diagnose what needs to change. This enables them to pinpoint the specific aspects of the organisation that need attention. To be able to see the wood for the trees is the challenge. In leadership theories, leaders are encouraged to take a 'canopy view' or to have 'helicopter vision'. What these phrases illustrate is the ability to rise above the current situation and to gain an overview.

Using Tools and Diagnostics

Sometimes leaders have an intuitive sense of what needs changing and are content to follow this; others find they are unable to rise above the current situation, can't see clearly and will benefit from a structured process to gain perspective. Using tools or diagnostics can be helpful in these cases. The McKinsey 7S model is one I recommend for establishing which aspect to focus on. By asking questions for each area, it's possible to use this model as a diagnostic.

When using such tools, involving people from different parts of the organisation to gain a rounded view is important. It's a simple enough process to build a survey using an on-line survey platform. This can also ensure confidentiality for respondents.

I've included a sample McKinsey Diagnostic for schools in the Appendix.

Richard Beckhard GRPI Model

Another useful tool is based on Richard Beckhard's GRPI model[27] (Goals, Roles, Processes and Interpersonal Relationships).

Beckhard believed that clarity of goals and roles, effective processes, and positive interactions and relationships were prerequisites for high-performing teams. I have used this model as a diagnostic to clarify how a team (or whole organisation) functions.

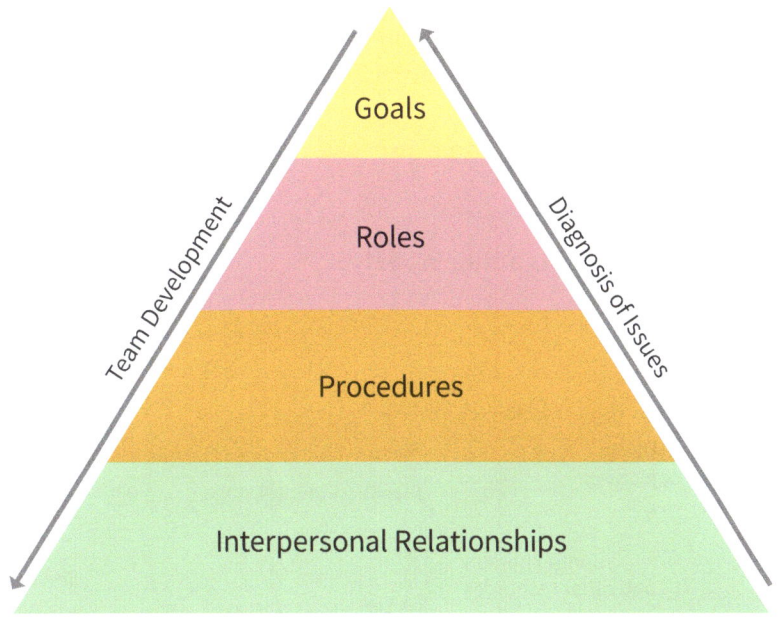

GRPI Model. Beckhard. 1972

One organisation I worked with was driven by relationships. It was a lovely place to work – however, it had lost its sense of vision and its goals were unclear. Beckhard's model was helpful in informing why this might be the case, as it illustrates a hierarchy meant to be followed downwards, with clarity of goal leading to specific roles, effective processes and then positive relationships. If turned upside down, where the starting point becomes great relationships, the processes may evolve to serve those relationships rather than the team's goals. People will adapt their roles to suit their strengths and preferences. If leaders don't challenge this, even when these roles do not actually serve the organisation best, eventually a lack of clear direction or vision prevents it from progressing.

STRATEGIC PLANNING

Once leaders know what needs to change, they must plan how to bring this about. Going back to Boyatzis' model, this is the learning agenda. Strategic planning gives the road map for change to happen. My own experience of developing strategy informs my writing as well as my work with other leaders. Strategic thinkers are blessed with the ability to plot a course toward goals and to consider the steps and challenges in between; strategic planning should involve others – leaders need to communicate with clarity, invite contributions and engage people's creativity.

I offer the following simple process on developing an effective strategy.

Sue Iqbal Strategic Planning Model [28]

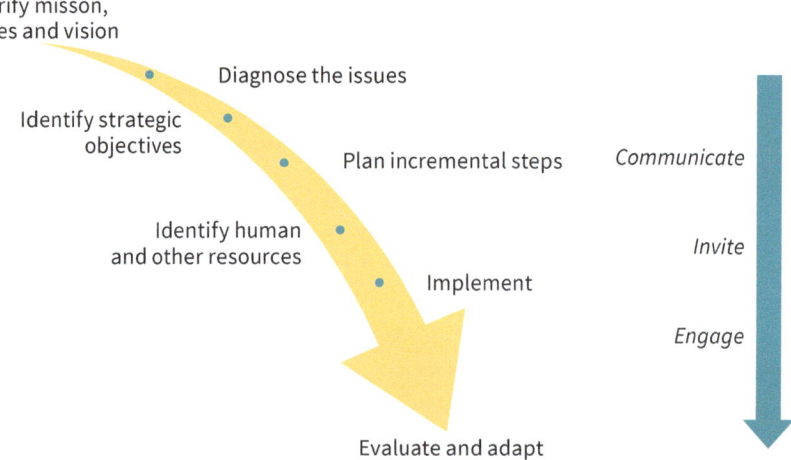

Alongside this process, leaders will need to be realistic about the challenges they face: opposition, lack of resources, external threats and their own strengths and weaknesses. As a coach, I have seen the power of 'holding up the mirror' to enable leaders to explore these challenges, and would recommend finding a skilled coach to support this process.

SWOT Model

SWOT

Tools such as SWOT analysis can inform this exploration.

It's unclear who created SWOT; it originated from the Stamford Research Institute and has been in widespread use since the 1960s/1970s. This tool works particularly well with groups of people, each participant contributing ideas and opinions. Used in this way, it's possible to discern how others view the situation. Some may look on threats as opportunities or see ways to turn weaknesses into strengths.

It's also likely that some will place more emphasis on weaknesses and threats. This may be an indication that these individuals will need help to see change positively.

SWOT analysis[29]

WORKING BELOW THE WATERLINE

Leaders need to recognise what may be happening in the realm of emotions, beliefs and values if they are to help people respond positively to change. Establishing the level of receptivity to change will enable leaders to have a realistic view of any resistance they may face, as well as to recognise the colleagues who will champion change.

Individuals resist change for a variety of reasons, including intellectual and rational disagreement, a challenge to belief and values, a perceived threat to identity or status, and fear of the unknown. Some personality types are more likely to want to preserve the status quo and others are energised by change. Leaders will need to carefully analyse the members of their teams and choose appropriate, and in some cases personalised, strategies for winning people over.

John Fisher Transition Curve Model

One model to help explain the emotional reaction to change that I've found helpful is the John Fisher Transition Curve, based on the Kubler-Ross model 1969[30] which explains the stages of grief in relation to dying. This has been adapted by John Fisher for the process of transition. The Fisher curve demonstrates the emotional reactions at different stages of change.

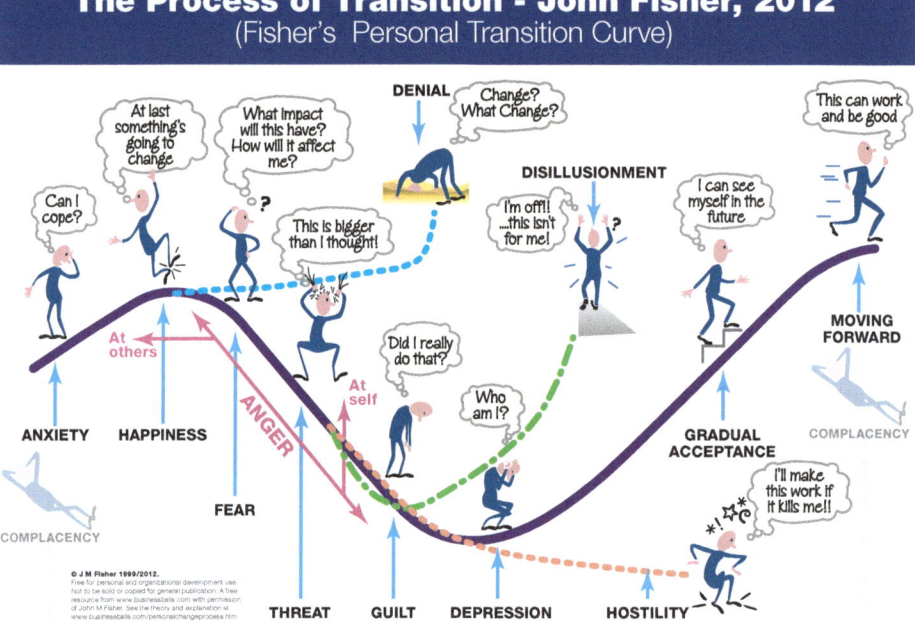

The Process of Transition – John Fisher[31]

One of my observations when working with organisations has been that the more frequent the change experienced, the more prolonged the collective emotional dip can become. Cynicism and initiative fatigue can grow, which inhibits the organisation's resilience to further change. Leaders need to assess their organisation's resilience to change by recognising the past journey and taking account of the current emotional temperature.

Working with schools that had experienced these prolonged periods of change, or frequent changes in leadership, I would facilitate a discussion using the Fisher curve model. This gave people the permission to accept and understand their emotional responses. Endeavouring to gain honest recognition and 'owning' of emotion enables an organisation to become emotionally literate and better prepared to confront issues below the waterline.

LEADERSHIP, SELF-AWARENESS AND EMOTIONAL INTELLIGENCE

For leaders to lead change well, they need to be self-aware, to reflect on their practice, have a range of leadership styles and to develop their emotional intelligence. As a coach, it is no surprise that I would recommend working with a coach who can help support a leader wishing to develop these qualities. I will briefly outline a tool to aid reflection and offer an introduction to Daniel Goleman's work on leadership style and emotional intelligence.

Reflective Practice

Leaders working below the waterline need to be able to reflect on the impact of their leadership style and behaviours. They should be able to articulate their personal values and see how these are consistently enacted in their practice. Colleagues are quick to notice inconsistency between what is said and what is done. Trust is built when these two things align. It is not an uncommon experience to replay the day's events over and over in one's mind. This can be helpful but often it is an unproductive act that leads to self-doubt. Choosing a more intentional and structured reflection can be more productive.

Sue Iqbal Process for Reflective Practice

The following process may be a helpful guide. I recommend taking time to undertake this practice on a regular basis, and would also suggest leaders work with a coach to support their reflection.[32]

Reflection Process

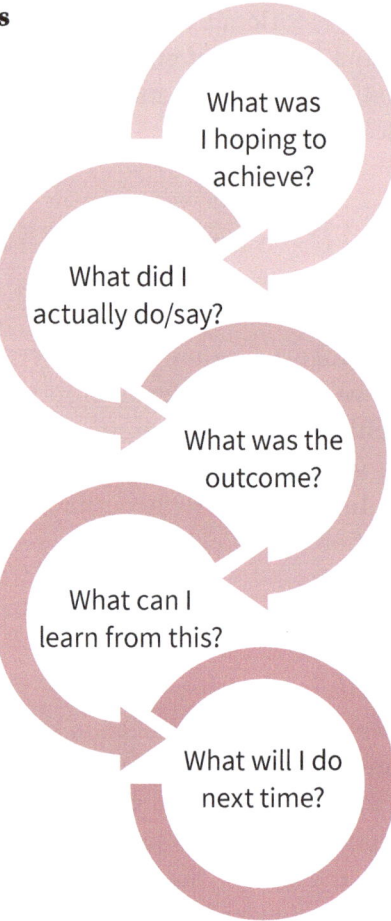

 Leadership Style Daniel Goleman

 Daniel Goleman: Leadership Style, Research and Theory

Daniel Goleman's work on leadership style and emotional intelligence was incorporated into the National College's leadership programmes and has been a useful resource that has shaped my thinking when developing leaders and creating leadership programmes. Goleman built on the work of George Litwin and Robert Stringer, who identified six styles of leadership in the 1960s. Their research looked at the impact of these styles on organisational climate. In my work with school leaders, I have noticed that the dominant leadership style will affect school culture because, as people respond to leadership behaviours, they in turn select behaviours that enable them to be rewarded or affirmed. As discussed in the chapter on climate creation, these reinforced behaviours become the way things are done. Leaders need to be intentional about their leadership style and aware of the impact it will have. Each style used in the right context will bring about results. However, if used in the wrong context the results can be counterproductive.

In *Leadership That Gets Results*[33], Harvard Business Review March/April 2000 Daniel Goleman writes about the impact of Leadership Styles on Climate and concludes that of the six leadership styles, Visionary leadership had the most positive effect on climate and affiliative, democratic and coaching follow close behind. In the same article the six styles are summarised:

Goldman's Six Leadership Styles
1. The coercive style. This "Do what I say" approach can be very effective in a turnaround situation, a natural disaster, or when working with problem employees. But in most situations, coercive leadership inhibits the organization's flexibility and dampens employees' motivation.

2. The authoritative style. An authoritative leader takes a "Come with me" approach: she states the overall goal but gives people the freedom to choose their own means of achieving it. This style works especially well when a business is adrift. It is less effective when the leader is working with a team of experts who are more experienced than he is.

3. The affiliative style. The hallmark of the affiliative leader is a "People come first" attitude. This style is particularly useful for building team harmony or increasing morale. But its exclusive focus on praise can allow poor performance to go uncorrected. Also, affiliative leaders rarely offer advice, which often leaves employees in a quandary.

4. The democratic style. This style's impact on organizational climate is not as high as you might imagine. By giving workers a voice in decisions, democratic leaders build organizational flexibility and responsibility and help generate fresh ideas. But sometimes the price is endless meetings and confused employees who feel leaderless.

5. The pacesetting style. A leader who sets high performance standards and exemplifies them himself has a very positive impact on employees who are self-motivated and highly competent. But other employees tend to feel overwhelmed by such a leader's demands for excellence—and to resent his tendency to take over a situation.

6. The coaching style. This style focuses more on personal development than on immediate work-related tasks. It works well when employees are already aware of their weaknesses and want to improve, but not when they are resistant to changing their ways.

Leaders will have preferred or natural styles, but effective leaders will learn the behaviours associated with the full range of styles and choose the most effective for a given situation or when working with a particular individual.

Developing an effective leadership toolkit does not mean that a leader who selects a behaviour for a specific situation is not being authentic; they are demonstrating the skill of differentiation. Teachers are brilliant at this; they will work differently with pupils dependent on their individual needs. Effective leadership requires the same flex.

Emotional Intelligence

Emotional Intelligence: Research and Theory
The New Leaders: Transforming the Art of Leadership by Goleman, Boyatzis and McKee explores the concept of primal leadership. They argue that a fundamental role of leaders is to prime good feeling in those they lead. This requires the leaders to be emotionally intelligent.

Emotional Intelligence has two domains, Personal Competence – how we manage ourselves: Self-Awareness and Self-Management and Social Competence, how we manage relationships: Social Awareness and Relationship Management. The Emotional Intelligence competencies as described by Goleman et al (page 39) are:

Self-Awareness
- Emotional self-awareness: Reading one's own emotions and recognising their impact; using gut sense to guide decisions
- Accurate self-assessment: Knowing one's own strengths and limits
- Self-confidence: A sound sense of one's self-worth and capabilities

Self-Management
- Emotional self-control: Keeping disruptive emotions and impulses under control
- Transparency: Displaying honesty and integrity; trustworthiness
- Adaptability: Flexibility in adapting to changing situations or overcoming obstacles
- Achievement: The drive to improve performance to meet inner standards of excellence
- Initiative: Readiness to act and seize opportunities
- Optimism: Seeing the upside in events

Social Awareness
- Empathy: Sensing others' emotions, understanding their perspective, and taking active interest in their concerns
- Organisational Awareness: Reading the currents, decision networks, and politics at the organisational level
- Service: Recognising and meeting follower, client, or customer needs

Relationship Management
- Inspirational leadership: Guiding and motivating with a compelling vision
- Influence: Wielding a range of tactics for persuasion
- Developing others: Bolstering others' abilities through feedback and guidance
- Change catalyst: Initiating, managing, and leading in a new direction
- Conflict management: Resolving disagreements
- Building bonds: Cultivating and maintaining a web of relationships
- Teamwork and collaboration: Cooperation and team building

Developing as an emotionally intelligent leader is personally challenging. It requires honest reflection and gaining feedback from others so that we can understand those aspects of our behaviours that are observed by others but often hidden to us, or that we prefer not to acknowledge. Working with a coach using a tool such as the **'Johari window'**[34] or getting **360-degree feedback** on leadership style using the **Hay Group (now Korn Ferry) Leadership Style Workbook**[35] can help expand our view of ourselves.

I have used and adapted questionnaires with many clients and have found that they enabled us to have a shared language for discussing leadership style and behaviours. Even when the results were challenging for the leader to receive, the resulting coaching session was able to go deeper and address some previously hidden areas. Emotionally intelligent leaders are brave and willing to confront their own weaknesses in order to become more effective.

In this chapter, I have outlined some building blocks for leading well. As I conclude, I urge leaders to keep the values uppermost in mind when leading change; to keep the integrity of practice aligned to those things that your organisation holds dear. This builds trust and your people will respect you for your integrity. However, it doesn't mean avoiding the hard decisions and actions of leadership. Restructuring may well require redundancy; difficult conversations will need to be held; unprofessional behaviour will have to be challenged. To undertake these actions, leaders need to be able to articulate the reason why they are required and to resolve to undertake them in ways which preserve dignity and demonstrate 'tough love'.

SACRED PERSPECTIVES ON LEADING WITH LOVE

I find much in the theories I have mentioned that resonates with my Christian beliefs. The description of emotional intelligence reflects some of the fruit of the Spirit. I can imagine Nehemiah in the Old Testament surveying the wreckage of Jerusalem's city walls, and using a SWOT or creating his strategy when faced with rebuilding. From the illustrations of leadership in the Bible, we see a clear, distinctive reliance on God for guidance, and His partnering with the leader in accomplishing the mission.

I have recently come across 'The Space for Grace Network',[36] led by Rick James and Elaine Vitikainen. Their work seeks to facilitate incorporating the spiritual dimension with best practice in organisational development. For Christian organisations and leaders, this approach intentionally invites God into the process of change.

When designing vision days for Christian organisations, I have given time for prayer, listening to what God may be saying both to individuals and collectively. This takes time and should not be rushed. One thing I have observed when doing this is that helping people notice what God is already doing and may be growing is often the key to discovering where

His heart is for the next season.

Change is God's agenda for individuals, organisations and nations. The Bible teaches much about personal change and urges us to be transformed by the renewing of our minds. This concept of sanctification is at the heart of discipleship. We are to become more like Christ, taking on His qualities but with the help of the Holy Spirit. The Bible also illustrates how God works through leaders to bring about change, partnering with Moses to bring the Israelites out of Egypt and, in the previous example, with Nehemiah to rebuild the walls of Jerusalem. In the Acts of the Apostles, we see the birth of the Early Church and, in the teaching of St Paul, how it can achieve its mission to bring change to individuals and live distinctly in community.

Jesus challenged people by highlighting the root causes of issues and exposing motivations, and He never shied away from going beneath the waterline. I love His relationship with Peter: He accepts Peter's impulsiveness when he jumps out of the boat to walk on the water; He acknowledges Peter's weaknesses and knows that he will betray Him. But in the end, Jesus offers grace to Peter and a way back into relationship. Peter is then transformed by the Holy Spirit into the leader on whom Jesus built His Church. Jesus must have seen this potential in the humble, impulsive fisherman and watched Peter grow. The transformation of Peter as a leader is inspiring; this is the work of the Holy Spirit.

I have been part of a prayer group for over 30 years. In this small group of four women, I've seen how God works with us as a gentle companion in challenging us to change. I have noticed that sometimes He highlights areas of weakness that He wants us to address. Often something will just 'come into the light', through a conversation or from a prayer, that brings about a particular emotional response. In this safe group of caring women, committed to walking life together, on no occasion have I seen God force us to change. Instead, I have seen the gentle work of His Spirit inviting, challenging, convicting, encouraging, equipping and providing so that we can change. I conclude from experience that God is in the business of change and He gently leads us forward. This is leading with love, and it is this example I believe leaders of people need to follow.

God's Love is Tough

In my life coaching work with individuals, I have observed that, as they seek to find their way through life, longing for God's best, a pattern emerges. Moving forwards towards a more fruitful life often requires the laying down of unhelpful but familiar patterns of thinking or behaviours. It's not possible even to imagine taking the next steps into a leadership role if the limiting belief you carry means you will not speak out the desire to be a leader, or your fear of failure is so great, you would rather not even begin the journey. In these situations, I have seen the effects of negative self-belief and strongholds of thought imprison individuals and prevent them from aspiring to their best life. I have also seen, with these same people, God's grace and love patiently giving them the courage to confront negative thinking, focus on truth and renew their minds.

God's love is not squishy and indulgent, allowing us to languish in our imprisonment; it is tough, requiring us to have courage to take the keys to break free and step forward.

'See, I am doing a new thing' (Isaiah 43:19): Loss and Change

As with any change, there is loss – therefore it often feels uncomfortable. We are used to the status quo. Even when we long to see God do a new thing, we hold on to the familiar. We stay in a job too long, even when we know it's not doing us any good. There are many reasons for this: we fear loss of financial security, status or role. In relationships, we collude with behaviours we don't like because to confront them requires us to speak out and risk rejection or conflict.

In coaching, there is an often-repeated phrase: if you do the things you have always done, you will get what you have always got. In our lives, to do the new thing, we have to say goodbye to the old. It can help us if we recognise and articulate the loss. Like any grief, it needs to be expressed in a healthy way. When I left teaching, I realised I would never go back into the classroom and my career path was taking a different direction. I wouldn't be a headteacher; I would no longer feel the joy of being part of a school family. These were losses I needed to recognise and mourn – not regret, but let go of. I could then embrace the new things God was leading me into.

Part 2: Enabling and Nurturing Outcomes

Chapter 6
INNOVATION

Key Concepts: Creativity

The Improving from WithIn model groups its six dimensions into two parts: the first three dimensions are the foundational tools with which to build an organisation; the second three are about nurturing the outcomes for thriving. The first of these dimensions for thriving is 'innovation'. In Improving from WithIn, innovation is about releasing the creativity in people to solve problems, make things better, master new skills, take risks, experiment and refine.

Human beings are naturally creative and, if we look at young children as they discover the world around them, we observe their innate curiosity, creativity and wonder. Many parents struggle with the frequent question 'why... ?' as their child seeks to understand and make sense of their experiences. Children appear to be hardwired for learning and creating.

As a parent, having only taught children with complex and challenging learning disabilities, for whom every learning experience needed to be scaffolded and planned, I was amazed when my own children appeared to learn without any intervention from me at all. When our children told us they were bored, my husband often said, 'It's good to be bored.' Frequently, a few minutes later, they had become absorbed in a new activity or had created a game from whatever was around the house or garden. In my visits to nursery and early years classrooms, I have seen how teachers harness innate curiosity and enable natural creativity to flourish.

What happens to children as they grow and mature is another extensive study, which I am unable to do justice to here. However,

I believe the progression to teenage years, the need to conform to the norms of peers, the effects of a knowledge-based school curriculum, acceptance of convention and the demands upon a workforce for compliance all contribute to quashing these innate gifts. My position is that, despite these constraining pressures, human beings, created in the image of a creative God, are themselves creative and able to innovate, design and create for pure joy and for the greater good of mankind and the world.

Writing this chapter during the COVID-19 lockdown of 2020, and seeing the effects of a pandemic as it threatened the human race, countries' health systems, economies and societies, I shared in the joy as humans mastered new communication methods and found ways to connect, sustain and inspire each other. I am in awe of the scientific minds that worked tirelessly to find breakthroughs to treat and combat the disease; the businesses that found different ways of working to ensure they survived; those able to future-gaze and anticipate trends that in the previous year would have seemed ridiculous. If ever there was a time to encourage innovation and creativity, it was then – just as it still is now.

The Latin word *innovare* means 'to make changes' or 'to do something differently' or, in the Cambridge Dictionary, 'a new idea or method'. With the challenges the world faces (climate change, limited resources, conflict and poverty), we need new ideas; we need to do things differently and to make changes that can enable a better world to emerge and thrive. Individual organisations must continually change and adapt to new challenges. Those able to innovate will be well placed to withstand changing circumstances.

Innovation relies upon creativity, the drive that is present in all humans and not just the domain of the arts world or the stereotypical creative personality. Creativity is defined as 'the ability to produce original and unusual ideas, or to make something new or imaginative' (Cambridge Dictionary). Many of the psychological studies into creativity focus on creative excellence or creative personality types, but fail to explore the universality of the human capacity to create. There are studies on the evolution of creativity, which explore the link between language, symbols and creative thought. These imply a universality of human capacity for creative thought and expression. Many explore humankind's early use of symbols, such as cave drawings, and the development of language and ability to communicate to others and to express thoughts and ideas. Visits to museums provide concrete evidence of our ancestors' abilities to create and develop tools to solve the problems they faced.

There is a debate about the need to include creativity in education, and a concern expressed by thought leaders such as Sir Ken Robinson that the education system is 'killing' creativity. His famous TED Talk from February 2006 explores this idea.

Durham University Research

The Durham Creativity Commission[37] is a collaboration between Arts Council England and Durham University, and aims to identify ways in which creativity – and specifically creative thinking – can play a larger part in our lives. Their research is focused on a wider definition of creativity. These quotes are from a post on The Conversation 16.10.18[38].

> On top of hobbies and interests, we all possess creative attributes that can help as we solve life's problems and make decisions. It is this type of creativity that enables us to plan different routes to get to the same destination, or how to fit in a trip to the supermarket when our schedule looks full.

> It might not sound very creative, but this aspect of creativity relies on our ability to consider options and assess their suitability, as well as how to make decisions based on personal prior experience or what we have learnt formally or informally. These examples are known as "small c creativity" or "personal everyday creativity".

> We are working alongside people in education, as well as businesses and arts and science communities, collecting their views on creativity and creative thinking. We will also be looking across these groups to determine whether or not there is a relationship between creativity and mobility, creativity and identity as well as creativity and well-being. We hope to be able to show that thinking creatively can not only be encouraged and furthered in a variety of contexts, but can also lead to positive outcomes on a personal, social and economic level.

The final report, published in October 2019, in which the recommendations are particularly focused on the education sector to impact on future generations, by enabling the development of creativity and creative thinking, can be read here: https://www.dur.ac.uk/creativitycommission/report/recommendations/

CREATIVITY TAKES MANY FORMS

Growing up, I never considered myself a creative person. I played the guitar and could just about strum and pluck my way through a song; I wrote poetry that was never shared with anyone but enabled me to express my feelings. Yet I have family members who are talented musicians, artistic and funny. My own mother was able to make a tailored winter coat with a fur-edged hood. If we measure our creativity through comparison with others who are more gifted, we will often conclude that we are not creative. I believed that too, until I realised that, give me a curriculum that needed to be created or a leadership programme that required designing – a set of ideas to communicate simply via a mental model – and I was in my element. My creative thinking was released.

In my work with young adults who had significant special needs, I appreciated the unique gifts and strengths each had. None were ever going to score highly academically or as artists or musicians, but amongst this group of young people, there was a comic, a gymnast, an escapologist, an empathetic friend and many who offered genuine love and warmth to others. Each had strengths and I noticed that, the more these strengths were fostered, the more able the student was to try to learn something new or accept greater challenges.

 Gardner Research on Multiple Intelligence

Howard Gardner and Positive Psychology on Human Strengths
Howard Gardner's research into multiple intelligence,[39] and Positive Psychology's collective work on the range of human strengths, recognise a broad spectrum of human gifts and offer an insight into the richness and diversity that these manifest within groups, organisations and communities. It is safe to conclude that our creativity will also express itself in diverse ways dependent upon these strengths. I believe in a philosophy for education that nurtures these God-given personal

gifts. As teachers and as parents, it is our job to help a child discover who they have been created to be as well as to acquire the skills and knowledge they will need to navigate the world. Applied to adults and to organisations, those who can harness the unique strengths and creative drives in all their members will benefit from innovations that contribute positively across the range of activities and functions.

Application in Organisations

Tools for Innovation and Creativity

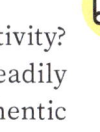

How then do organisations encourage innovation and nurture creativity? Research into how successful companies foster innovation is readily available. Much of it echoes my focus on purpose, values, authentic leadership behaviours and helpful processes leaders can engage in that will support an innovative culture.

LEADERS SEEKING TO NURTURE INNOVATION CAN:

1. **Values**
   a. Make explicit that innovation, experimentation, and creativity are valued in your organisation
   b. Reward these behaviours

2. **Leadership**
   a. Ensure leaders demonstrate behaviours that encourage contributions from all at every level in the organisation
   b. Provide psychological safety by consistent reinforcement of values
   c. Grow 'intellectual trust' and develop competence
   d. Restructure away from hierarchical model
   e. Invest in leadership at all levels

3. **Cultural Practice**
   a. Encourage widespread use of open questions
   b. Remove blame and develop positive strategies to accept and learn from failure
   c. Accept new ideas may need refining, reward perseverance
   d. Give space and time for creative thinking
   e. Use professional development for ideas generation
   f. Constructively challenge and explore possibilities
   g. Look outwards and find good practice and ideas
   h. Encourage co-creation and synergy by working with others

Problem-Solving as Catalyst

Often the stimulus for innovation is the need to solve a problem or improve something. Members within an organisation can often see solutions and are willing to try out new ideas to meet these challenges. The motivation to make things better is a strong one; Dan Pink, in his work *Drive*, argues that it is one of the top three drivers. For people to find satisfaction, they need to know that their work matters and that it is contributing to the greater good. Leaders need to communicate both the need for innovation and that the work to find solutions and new ideas is contributing to the purpose or mission – which in turn will make the world a better place.

One primary school I worked with was seeking to involve parents and their community, and to work across its partner schools and the community services sharing the site. The headteacher offered young middle leaders the opportunity of time to invest in finding ways to do this. Over a period of months, I facilitated their exploration of the challenges and the good practice that existed in a neighbouring region, visioning and generating ideas. This opportunity was not about developing young leaders from a deficit model or, as is often the case, re-educating where senior leaders consider there are problems. It was a generous provision of time and resources, given in the belief that these young leaders would use it well; they would grow in confidence and the school would benefit in finding solutions.

I have also seen leaders crush innovation and creative thinking, staff members afraid to take ideas to their managers for fear of not being listened to, or those who are discouraged by the response, 'That won't work here' or, 'We tried that before and it failed'. Sadly, in these situations the culture discourages and the natural reaction can often be to close down creativity or to confine it to interests outside work. This reduces the potential not just for the individual but also for their contribution in the organisation. Continual discouragement can erode even the most confident people. Some will stay put, frustrated and increasingly prone to negativity; others will leave, taking their wounds elsewhere, and it may take a long time for their creative thinking to reignite. I believe this is because, to innovate and think creatively, we are taking the risk of ploughing new ground; we are giving something of ourselves; we risk failure or rejection. If there is not psychological safety, we often adopt defensive behaviours, which in turn affect the climate and can reinforce a negative culture. This diminishes everyone.

INNOVATION IN CHURCH

Rick Warren Tool for Innovation in Church
While thinking how innovation may apply to church leadership, I came across this blog from Rick Warren on Pastors.com[40]. Clearly Rick Warren and I share common ground on this subject.

> **6 Ways to Create a Culture of Innovation in Your Church**
> Creativity matters in ministry. It matters because God is creative. He's the most creative being in the entire universe. It only makes sense that we serve God with our creativity.
>
> How do you develop a culture of innovation in your church?
>
> **You need a theology of innovation.** We are most like our creator when we're creative. God wired us to be creative. Children are very creative. They are born creative. It's normal. We get the creativity kicked out of us as time goes by. We learn to be afraid. But a theology of innovation always reminds us that God intends us to be creative.
>
> **You need a creative atmosphere.** There are certain environments I can be very creative in, and certain environments where I can't. At Saddleback, we've never had a boardroom or the big boardroom-style table that comes with that. We have recliners. Meetings don't start at Saddleback until we kick our feet up. It's when I get in a totally prone position that I can be the most creative and can discover what God would have us do.
>
> **You need to stay playful.** Playfulness stimulates creativity. When you get people laughing, you get the endorphins going. Creativity is often putting together two exactly opposite ideas, which is often ludicrous or seemingly stupid. It just makes people laugh. When people start to laugh, I know creativity is coming. When they're serious, we're not going to get creative.
>
> **You need the freedom to fail.** Innovation means not being afraid to fail. There's no such thing as failure at Saddleback. We experiment. Sometimes we guess. It's trial and error. But I give

my staff the freedom and flexibility to fail. You're never a failure at Saddleback until you stop trying. We've done more things that didn't work than did. I want all of my staff members to make at least one mistake a week. If they aren't making mistakes, they aren't trying!

You need to think big! You foster innovation by setting goals that are so big that you are bound to fail unless God bails you out. We did this before we started 40 Days of Purpose back in 2002. We had been planning to start 300 new small groups through the campaign. That would have been a big deal. But God told me, "Add a zero. Start 3,000 small groups." But we didn't have 3,000 small group leaders. So we innovated. We came up with a brand new way to do small groups, as we focused on finding "hosts" instead of leaders.

You must do something that matters. My friend, Erwin McManus, once told me, "The reality is that if you're not trying to accomplish something meaningful, you're not really being pressed into the creative process." We don't innovate at Saddleback to be cool. We innovate because we want to reach people with the good news about Jesus. The why determines what we do.

Context and Innovation

The value placed on innovation in an organisation may depend upon openness to new ideas by individual leaders, but it also may reflect the prevailing view of the sector within which they operate. In the business community, innovation may be welcomed as a means to stay ahead, have a competitive edge or create new products. As a result, it is highly valued. In education, innovation is sometimes resisted as it does not flourish well in a culture of prescription.

The arrival of a global pandemic stimulated a quiet revolution of technological innovation in the teaching profession, harnessing the creative gifts of teachers in using online platforms to teach remotely. In the Church, a similar explosion of virtual activities took place, the reach of which surprised many who had worked within the confines of church buildings and had counted face-to-face attendance as a measure of success. Watching and participating in beautiful spiritual acts such as the UK Blessing, a virtual service for Pentecost hosted by the Archbishop of Canterbury and involving the Pope, and virtual church services, I wondered at the ability of human beings to be creative and to partner with God to bring good in all circumstances.

SACRED PERSPECTIVE ON INNOVATION AND CREATIVITY

Created in the Likeness of a Creator God
The creation story in Genesis lays the foundation for expectation that human beings, created in the image of Creator God, will be capable of creative acts, thoughts and innovation. Rereading the account of God's commission for Adam to participate with Him in creation, both by naming the animals and by taking care of the created world, I was struck again by the heart of God for partnering with humans to bring about His purposes in the world He has created.

Creativity in Man Harnessed for God's Purposes
In the story of the building of the tent of meeting in Exodus 31, God chooses Bezalel to be filled with His Spirit to gift him skills, ability and knowledge in all kinds of crafts. Along with Oholiab and an unnamed group of craftspeople, Bezalel works to creatively interpret the instructions of God to make beautiful and sacred things, using materials such as precious metals and stones. All this reflects beauty and inspires awe. Here, we see God inspiring people with purpose, gifting them with creative skills and, in turn, partnering in the act of co-creation to further His kingdom.

Creation Inspiring Worship as a Reflection of God
Throughout the Psalms, the created world is both the inspiration for worship and a reminder of the greatness of Creator God. The created points to the Creator, its beauty, magnificence, intricate detail and complexity all inspiring worship. Appreciation of the natural world frequently arouses responses of emotion and a sense of transcendence. It is often in looking at the created that eminent scientists conclude there must have been a higher being at work in the creation and evolution of the world; it cannot have just been an accident.

Jesus' Creative Ministry

I love the accounts of Jesus' ministry: His creative teaching, use of stories and metaphor are all to communicate a deeper truth. This aspect of Jesus' life particularly resonates with the teacher in me. The images He uses to illustrate and teach are usually based on everyday objects or familiar situations, the result being that His audience understood His message. Jesus used His creative communication to point to the nature of His Father God.

The other lesson I take from Jesus' ministry is that creativity takes different forms. We don't know what sort of carpenter He was, but we do know He was a creative teacher.

Throughout the Bible, there are illustrations of people individually gifted in unique ways, all of whom are called to contribute to furthering God's kingdom.

Called To Create in Building The Kingdom

When we look back through history, we can see creative gifts harnessed to build places of worship; inspiring works of art; music that evokes transcendence; acts of service that transform communities, and application of scientific innovation to bring about healing. As human beings, we are inspired to use our gifts for a higher purpose and to continue to partner with God to bring about His kingdom. This universal call to align our gifts to God's purposes for our lives, and in turn to experience fruitfulness, is summed up for me in the words of the psalmist in Psalm 1:

> Blessed is the man who does not walk in the counsel of the wicked or stand in the way of sinners or sit in the seat of mockers.
> But his delight is in the law of the Lord and on his law he meditates day and night.
> He is like a tree planted by streams of water which yields its fruit in season and whose leaf does not wither.
> Whatever he does prospers. (Psalm 1:1-3)

Here, the call for integrity and heart alignment to God's law, nourished by living water, brings about fruitfulness that lasts. For all of us – created in His image, aligned to His purposes, using the gifts He has deposited in us – we have the potential to be fruitful and to use our unique creativity to innovate and bring prosperity to our world.

Chapter 7
MOTIVATION

Key Theories: Maslow, McClelland, Pink

The second dimension on the outcomes side of the Improving from WithIn model is motivation. Human beings thrive when they are motivated. There is an energy that is released when motivation is present; it drives us forward towards goals or away from negative or harmful forces.

Motivation can be positive or negative. It can also be intrinsic or extrinsic: an internal state where we're attracted towards something, or we're driven towards an external goal to meet our needs. We are complex; motives or drivers, often subconscious, ensure we get our needs met. Grouped into 'basic' – hunger, thirst, sex, avoidance of pain, fear – or 'secondary' – achievement, power or social – these needs impact on the choices we make and the behaviours we engage in.

Human motivational theories seek to explain the force of motivation. The word itself is derived from the word 'motive', a reason for a person to act, and from the Latin 'motivus', from 'movere', meaning 'to move'. Motivation is a powerful force that we need to understand before we can look at its application in Improving from WithIn.

HUMAN MOTIVATION THEORIES

Abraham Maslow

In my college days, I learned about Maslow's Hierarchy of Needs, one of the early theories of motivation. It is still cited as foundational thinking on the subject, and contributes to our understanding of how physiological and safety needs – 'deficiency needs' – are required to be met before belonging, self-esteem and self-actualisation – 'growth needs' – can be realised.

Abraham Maslow, a psychologist, wrote a paper in 1943, *A Theory of Human Motivation*.[41] His theory proposed that humans were motivated by their needs, organised into a hierarchy. We move on to the higher needs only when the lower or basic needs have been met. Modern-day psychologists now believe that the hierarchy is not incremental but more fluid. However, Maslow's theory is still respected and has contributed to the field of positive psychology.

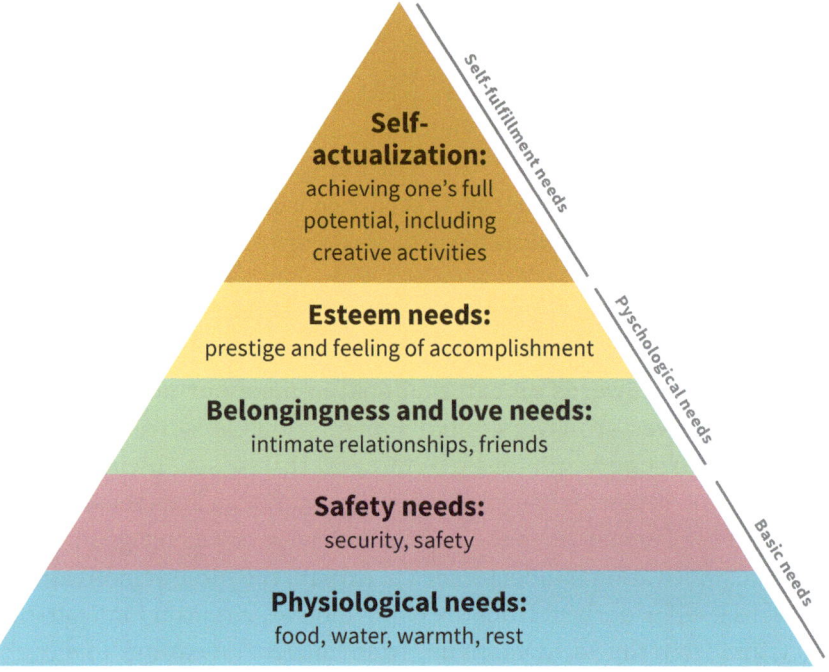

In 2017, I worked on a project to tackle educational underachievement in Warwickshire primary schools. Much of our work was focused on children whose life experiences meant that some of their physiological, safety and psychological needs had not been met, either recently or at a key point in their development. Unsurprisingly, these children found it more difficult to learn, to develop healthy self-esteem or aspire to achieve their potential. As we worked together to develop strategies to address some of the 'basic' or, as Maslow would define them, 'lower order' needs, teachers recognised the importance of working beyond the school walls. They needed to consider the whole life experience of the child and access support from family and community, as well as ensuring the children felt safe in school. As a result of teachers taking this holistic approach, the children were better able to engage in learning. Maslow's hierarchy is well known in the education profession and it informed our discussions.

I had symptoms of COVID-19 and had to self-isolate, I was unable to access food delivery from a supermarket, I felt very unsafe and anxious. Meeting my basic needs and those of my family was going to be a challenge. Furthermore when the toilet flush broke and I could not repair it myself, I became incredibly stressed. In that state, I could not concentrate on anything else and definitely hadn't the capacity for writing or coaching others until I knew how these needs would be met. Yet as these needs began to be met, often by the kindness of neighbours, the panic subsided and strategies for coping were established. I noticed I began to have a renewed capacity to engage.

David McClelland

Another helpful model was proposed by David McClelland, a psychologist working at Harvard in the 1950s. McClelland published his model of human motivation in his book, *The Achieving Society*.[42] He proposed that three dominant needs – for achievement, for power and for affiliation – underpin human motivation. He believed that, although we have all three drivers, one will be more dominant dependent upon our cultural context and experience. These drivers will shape our defining characteristics. So, a person with the achievement driver is likely to set and accomplish challenging goals; with affiliation, to want to belong and collaborate rather than compete; with power, to want to lead, enjoy status and seek to influence others, and they are more likely to compete. McClelland's work is particularly applicable in understanding how people operate in a work or group context. Both his work and similar studies have informed the research and provided tools to help to understand personality and leadership styles. The use of such tools supports greater self-awareness.

I use tools like this in my leadership coaching work and have found them to be particularly helpful in unpicking the main drivers in senior teams. One such team was comprised of individuals all scoring highly for the affiliative driver. The impact of this was great for harmony and creating a positive climate but not so helpful for agreeing a strategic direction. In time, this led to frustration in moving forwards. Understanding the impact of the affiliative driver enabled greater clarity about the dynamics at play in the team and subsequently led to finding more effective ways of operating.

In another organisation, the leader was driven by power. He created strong, decisive leadership and led from the front; he was effective and inspired followership. However, he questioned how to grow a sustainable team around him. Understanding the impact of his drivers and leadership style enabled him to consider new leadership behaviours to encourage his team to become less dependent and to grow their own leadership confidence.

These two theories (Maslow and McClelland) resonated with me and have informed my work, as well as providing a background to understanding the study of motivation. The field is developing rapidly especially as understanding in neuroscience grows. These early studies have been built on and have become more accessible to non-academics. Much is available via TED talks and in non-academic literature. In 2010, I picked up one such book by Daniel H. Pink, which would help crystallise my thinking and create the impetus for Improving from WithIn.

Dan Pink: *Drive*

Drive: The Surprising Truth About What Motivates Us by Daniel H. Pink was published in 2009.[43] Dan Pink, an American author from a law, economics and politics background, is now a sought-after thinker and speaker. *Drive* is an accessible yet serious study into the area of intrinsic motivation. Pink addresses the impact of target-driven systems on human motivation, providing a scientifically based case for the need to foster intrinsic motivation to enable complex cognitive tasks and creative thought to flourish. Pink argues that reward systems and targets, although effective for simple and repetitive tasks, can actually impede the ability of humans to perform more complex and self-directed activities.

Citing research by Howard F. Harlow in the late 1940s and further developed by Edward Deci and Richard Ryan[44] in the 1970s, he explores the science behind the drive which became known as 'intrinsic motivation'. Deci and Ryan, psychologists at Rochester University, proposed self-determination theory. They argued that humans have innate psychological needs: competence, autonomy and relatedness. These form the basis for Pink's model, which he names, Autonomy, Mastery and Purpose. Pink quoting a conversation with Ryan, 'If there is anything (fundamental) about our nature, it's the capacity for interest'[45]. These studies have led psychologists to conclude that human beings engage in activities for their own sake, not just to gain a reward, to meet physiological needs or to avoid danger.

Mihaly Csikszentmihalyi[46] is a Hungarian–American psychologist and one of the founders of the Positive Psychology movement. In his study of creativity and play, he observed painters so enthralled in what they were doing that they were unaware of time passing. When in this highly focused mental state, we are 'lost' or caught up in an activity, the activity itself being rewarding. He later described this state as being 'in flow'.

This study provided Pink with a compelling case for challenging the way business and society reward workers in an ever more complex world, where simple tasks are increasingly undertaken by technology, and humans endeavour to solve complex problems that require innovative, creative and complex cognitive solutions. The current target-driven economies and political policies can be impeding our abilities to think beyond those targets and to release our imaginations. Echoing Deci and Ryan, Pink argues that intrinsic motivation is fragile; for humans to flourish, their drive for autonomy, mastery and purpose needs to be recognised and encouraged.

Reading *Drive* was a lightbulb moment for me. Reflecting on the impact of targets on morale in the education sector and talking to leaders from other settings, I could see the effect policy was having. My understanding of positive psychology, organisational development and leadership theories had made me question current practice, and Pink's argument in *Drive* became the last piece of the jigsaw. When it fell into place, it spurred me on to consider, *if these things are true, there must be a better way to do it.* From this, Improving from WithIn was born.

I believe society needs our organisations and the people within them to thrive; we need humans to be able to undertake complex and creative thinking to find solutions to the challenges we all face. In return, our organisations and those who set policy will need to understand how to foster and release intrinsic motivation.

It will be helpful to consider Pink's drivers – autonomy, mastery and purpose – in a little more detail. Deci and Ryan write, 'Autonomous motivation involves behaving with a full sense of volition or choice.' This is different from independence or individualism; it is about acting with choice.

Pink writes, 'Researchers have found a link between autonomy and overall well-being.' Citing recent science studies he adds, 'Autonomous motivation promotes greater conceptual understanding, better grades, enhanced persistence at school, higher productivity, less burnout, and greater levels of psychological wellbeing. These are also seen in the workplace.'[47]

Mastery is about getting better at something: learning new skills, perfecting performance. It requires a positive 'can do' or growth mindset (Carol Dweck).[48] It also requires perseverance. Carol Dweck comments, 'Effort is one of the things that gives meaning to life. Effort means that you care about something, that something is important to you, and you are willing to work for it. It would be an impoverished existence if you were not willing to value things and commit yourself to working towards them.'[49] Regarding the third element of purpose, Pink writes, 'Autonomous people working toward mastery perform at very high levels. But those that do so in the service of some higher objective can achieve even more.'[50] Mihaly Csiksentmihalyi has said in an interview with Pink, 'Purpose provides activation energy for living. I think that evolution has had a hand in selecting people who had a sense of doing something beyond themselves.'[51]

I have seen evidence of all three drivers in the people I have coached: the need to find their own way forward, to make choices and become more autonomous. I have also seen the impact of over-prescription in quashing this drive. I love to see my clients learning or improving their skills and working towards goals they have set, and being energised more than they were when goals were externally imposed. Seeking to make the world a better place is a compelling drive. As we each find our personal call to work towards a higher purpose, we are enabled to accomplish extraordinary things.

Like Pink, I conclude that science and wisdom are sending a strong message to rethink the way we use targets and rewards, so that people can really thrive and solve the problems we all face. Releasing the intrinsic motivational drive is vital to achieving this.

Motivation: A Word of Caution

Motivation, as we have seen, is comprised of powerful drives that ensure we get our needs met. Unchecked, it has the potential to be individualistic and selfish. In some people, where pain and hurt lie at the root of behaviours, getting needs met may mean overriding others in the thoughtless pursuit of them. This can be toxic; the drive for achievement can play out as workaholism, stepping on others to rise in the workplace or engaging in unsafe or illegal practice to achieve.

Power can be wielded for the sake of it. It can be addictive and power addicts can use it to feed their need for status. This can even play out in manipulative ways, where the powerful person controls others, or makes them vulnerable so as to maintain their position of dominance.

The need for affiliation can cause a person to be liked or needed by others to a point where dependency develops. It can equally damage the person seeking affiliation, as they underplay their own desires to appear likable. However, resentment can fester and eventually damage the relationship.

Application in Organisations

It is clear from the research that motivated people are more productive, have a better sense of wellbeing and are more able to make a positive contribution to an organisation. Leaders create the environment where motivation thrives or withers; they have the power to be intentional, implementing strategies that encourage, as well as noticing and intervening where motivation is lacking.

Tool: Increasing Motivation

How to Increase Motivation

Leaders seeking to increase motivation can:
- *Make provision so basic needs are met*
    - Ensure safe practice
    - Meet physiological needs, access to regular breaks, food, hygiene facilities etc
    - Have a fair, transparent, and equitable pay policy

- *Value social interaction and relationships*
    - Invest in social activities
    - Encourage collaboration
    - Talk to staff members and find out about their lives and what matters to them
    - Have an open door policy

- *Attend to psychological needs*
    - Create a psychologically safe climate
    - Challenge and address unprofessional behaviour
    - Consistently model behaviours aligned to values

- Encourage and listen to others
- Develop mental health awareness

- *Build people up*
  - Have an active strategy for professional development
  - Actively develop leadership skills and self-awareness
  - Notice talent and find ways to give opportunities for using it
  - Give regular and specific feedback
  - Develop coaching and mentoring across the organisation (include coaching across departments and levels of seniority)
  - Make timely interventions when someone is struggling to perform well (find out why)

- *Develop autonomy*
  - Understand the impact of your leadership style on others
  - Give clarity about job remits
    - + Role
    - + Responsibility
    - + Relationships
    - + Resources
  - Seek ways to give ownership to others
  - Share the problems that need solving and give time for others to find solutions
  - Offer 'free development time' as part of regular professional development cycle
  - Use coaching style to invite others to find solutions

- *Foster mastery and learning*
  - Invest in the development of staff
  - Encourage people to identify learning needs and find resources to support them
  - Demonstrate own learning and create a culture where it is encouraged
  - Find platforms for people to share and shine

- *Make purpose explicit*
  - Champion the purpose of the organisation
  - Keep values visible
  - Recruit in line with purpose and values

SACRED PERSPECTIVES ON MOTIVATION

Motivation is why we act and what we act on. As human beings, we have the drivers to survive and have our relational and psychological needs met. Our motives can be self-centred purely to ensure we satisfy these drivers. Or, if rooted in gratitude for the grace we have received from God, they can become the force for serving Him in all we do and for what we focus our energies on. The Bible teaches us to renew our minds. In doing this, we surrender both our hearts and minds to scrutiny by the Holy Spirit, to convict us, teach us, renew us and help us bear His fruit.

Jesus teaches us that the greatest commandment is to love one another. This is to be our response from first receiving God's love. Our deepest need to be accepted by and in relationship with Father God now satisfied, we, in turn, motivated by love, seek to act in love towards others. We seek to serve God and build His kingdom.

In 1 John chapter 4, we are taught that love comes from God, who is Himself love. He first loved us and, having received this love, we then love others. This is our motivation.

> Dear friends, let us love one another, for love comes from God. Everyone who loves has been born of God and knows God. Whoever does not love does not know God, because God is love. This is how God showed his love among us: he sent his one and only Son into the world that we might live through him. This is love: not that we loved God, but that he loved us and sent his Son as an atoning sacrifice for our sins. Dear friends, since God so loved us, we also ought to love one another. No one has ever seen God; but if we love one another, God lives in us and his love is made complete in us.
>
> This is how we know that we live in him and he in us: he has given us of his Spirit. And we have seen and testify that the Father has sent his Son to be the Saviour of the world. If anyone acknowledges that Jesus is the Son of God, God lives in them and they in God. And so we know and rely on the love God has for us.
>
> God is love. Whoever lives in love lives in God, and God in them. This is how love is made complete among us so that we will have confidence on the day of judgment: in this world we are like Jesus. There is no fear in love. But perfect love drives

out fear, because fear has to do with punishment. The one who fears is not made perfect in love.

We love because he first loved us. Whoever claims to love God yet hates a brother or sister is a liar. For whoever does not love their brother and sister, whom they have seen, cannot love God, whom they have not seen. And he has given us this command: anyone who loves God must also love their brother and sister. (1 John 4:7–21)

When my children were little, I would go into their rooms when they were sleeping, just to look at them; and I would experience an overwhelming emotion of love. They were doing nothing to earn that love; not being good or trying hard or learning something; just simply 'being'. I would tell them that God's love is like that. Our experience as Christians is that, despite receiving God's love, we still seek to feel acceptable or significant somehow. We struggle to really believe we are loved and, as a result, can enter into a cycle of behaviours that diminish the freedom God's love should give us.

When involved in the Church School Leadership programme, I learned the Dynamic Cycle of Grace, developed by Frank Lake and Dr Emil Brunner.[52] I find this model fascinating as it helps to explain the difference grace should make to our motives, and how true acceptance from God can release us from striving.

The Dynamic Cycle: Frank Lake and Dr Emil Brunner

We are familiar with the pressure to achieve in order to feel significant or have a sense of self-worth. This leads us to strive to keep performing and to achieve more, and we feel a sense of failure when things go wrong. If our status is damaged, we can experience emotions of rejection or loss.

The Dynamic Cycle challenges this view. It starts with acceptance: before we can achieve, we need to feel accepted. Acceptance then enables us to be nourished and sustained, and from this arises our sense of significance. Lake believed that, in healthy childhoods, a child experiences acceptance: they are sustained by love and nourishment from their family, and this sustains them in achieving and overcoming the challenges of reaching adulthood.

Lake also believed that this cycle reflects the relationship Jesus had with Father God and is available to followers of Christ. The model challenges the current culture of achievement and, for many who have experienced the pressure of modern culture as well as imperfect parenting, it provides hope that, by acknowledging our acceptance by God, we can experience freedom from striving to achieve. We are sustained by God's ongoing love and, out of this gift by grace, we are motivated to act and to seek to serve Him.

Dynamic Cycle of Grace

Contrast with the Cycle of Frustration

We feel the need to achieve in order to gain our sense of significance or status, and this has to be continually reinforced so that we feel accepted.

We can see the impact of this cycle in our lives and the culture we live in underlines it: we keep driving ourselves to meet our need for acceptance by achieving or doing more. When we fail or fall short of the goals we have set ourselves, we experience negative emotions and lose our sense of self-worth.

One famous example of this is encapsulated by the pop icon Madonna in 1991, in an interview in *Vanity Fair*:[53]

And all of my will has always been to conquer some horrible feeling of inadequacy. I'm always struggling with that fear. I push past one spell of it and discover myself as a special human being and then I get to another stage and think I'm mediocre and uninteresting. And I find a way to get myself out of that. Again and again. My drive in life is from this horrible fear of being mediocre. And that's always pushing me, pushing me.

This cycle, when played out in our lives, leads to burnout and stress. We need to reset our minds and counter our cultural experience with the Dynamic Cycle of Grace, a model which powerfully reflects my own experience of gazing at my sleeping children. The gospel teaches us that we are unconditionally loved and accepted. From that position – not earned but by grace – we in turn, motivated by love, seek to serve: 'For we are God's handiwork, created in Christ Jesus to do good works, which God prepared in advance for us to do' (Ephesians 2:10).

Chapter 8
ENGAGEMENT

Key Concepts: Wellbeing, Flow, Strengths, Performance, Flourishing

When human beings are motivated, they become engaged; when they are engaged, deep learning and high performance take place. In organisations with high levels of engagement, a climate of meaningful purpose develops, along with the behaviours associated with going the extra mile and a generosity of spirit.

In positive psychology, engagement is seen to be a state of activation in which emotions, cognition and behaviour are all involved. It is in this heightened or activated state that human beings perform and learn best, invest in activities, reach their potential and thrive. For these reasons, much of the research into organisational health and with high-performing companies has focused on and measured engagement in the workforce.

There are other definitions of engagement. These all point to a relationship or a connection with something, an idea or someone. Engagement is not passive; it is a heightened state that involves our emotions, physiology, spirituality and cognition. In this chapter, I will argue that organisations which invest in and nurture the engagement of their employees will flourish.

Seligman's Theory of Well-Being

Martin Seligman's PERMA Theory of Well-Being[54] sees engagement as one of the five core elements or building blocks of human flourishing. Engagement is linked to the concept of flow. When our need for engagement is met with an activity, we experience a release of positive neurotransmitters and hormones that elevate our sense of wellbeing. This engagement helps us remain present and focused. We experience positive emotions, such as calm or joy. Engagement is deeply personal; it relates to our strengths and passions and we need it for our overall wellbeing.

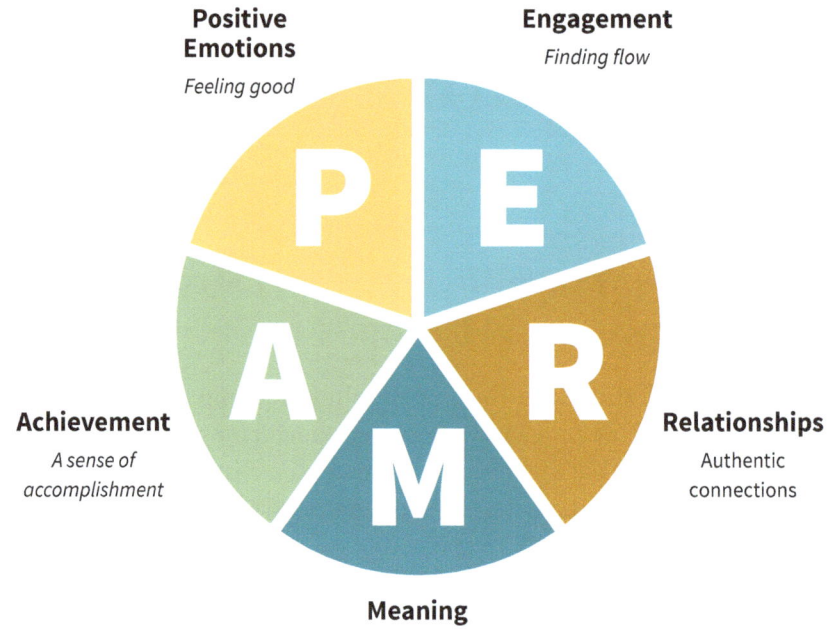

Positive Psychology.com[55]

Employee Engagement

RESEARCH INTO EMPLOYEE ENGAGEMENT

Kingston University Business School published a literature review of Employee Engagement in a Working Paper by Sandeep Kular, Mark Gatenby, Chris Rees, Emma Soane and Katie Truss.[56] I recommend it as a helpful overview of the history of research in this field. I found this paper affirming because the research highlights much of what I have been saying in this book: it links engagement with flow and provides a case for giving employees opportunities for autonomy and to innovate. Additionally, it backs up my belief that psychological safety is critical in organisations, and the case for strong and effective leadership is made. This is important to me because in my own learning style, reflected in the process of creating Improving from WithIn, I have learned to trust my intuition. I often know something in my 'knower'. I build on previous knowledge and experience, which is then outworked and developed by talking with others and researching the existing theories and research base. I have been reassured to find that my thinking is backed up by respected investigation.

In the Kingston paper, the work of William Kahn is cited. Kahn was the first to formally define employee engagement as 'the harnessing of organisation members' selves to their work roles; in engagement, people employ and express themselves physically, cognitively, and emotionally during role performances'.

The cognitive aspect of employee engagement concerns employees' beliefs about the organisation, its leaders and working conditions; the emotional aspect concerns how employees feel about each of those three factors, and whether they have positive or negative attitudes towards the organisation and its leaders; the physical aspect of employee engagement concerns the physical energies exerted by individuals to accomplish their roles. Thus, according to Kahn,[57] engagement means to be psychologically as well as physically present when occupying and performing an organisational role. Kular et al. Truss et al 2006[58] define engagement simply as 'passion for work'. In his book, *Leadership in Organisations*, Professor John Storey gives a further definition: 'A set of positive attitudes and behaviours enabling high job performance of a kind which are in tune with the organisation's mission.'[59]

In 2009, the 'Engaging for Success' Report by David McLeod and Nita Clarke was published, having been commissioned the previous year by John Hutton MP, the then Secretary of State for Business.[60] The report takes an in-depth look at employee engagement and the potential benefits for business.

In his introduction, Lord Mandelson writes:

> This timely Report sets out for the first time the evidence that underpins what we all know intuitively, which is that only organisations that truly engage and inspire their employees produce world class levels of innovation, productivity and performance.

> The authors, in their own introduction, state that one of their aspirations for the report is for it to be 'about unlocking people's potential at work and the measurable benefits of doing so for the individual, the organisation and, ultimately, for the UK'.

Addressing the issue of defining 'engagement', the report suggests the following: 'We believe it is most helpful to see employee engagement as a workplace approach designed to ensure that employees are committed to their organisation's goals and values, motivated to contribute to organisational success, and are able at the same time to enhance their own sense of well-being.' (Page 9)

The report evidences the correlation between employee engagement and performance, innovation and wellbeing. It identifies four main enablers to greater employee engagement. I summarise these below:

Leadership – a strong narrative about the purpose, aims and values of the organisation.
Engaging Managers – a culture of facilitating and empowering staff rather than directing.
Voice – strategies to listen to and give employees a voice.
Integrity – behaviour that is consistent to the values.

This research echoes much of my basis for Improving from WithIn on and affirms my thinking. It does, however, point out that engagement levels in the UK were low at the point when the report was written, following the recession of 2008. After years of austerity, the COVID-19 pandemic and further economic turmoil, I can only conclude that this may still be the case.

ENGAGEMENT, STRENGTHS AND FLOW

The other aspect of engagement I want to explore here is the work that has risen from positive psychology on the benefits for individuals of finding their place of 'flow' and understanding their personal strengths. My coaching clients often come to me without really understanding their unique make-up and, as a result, can be unable to make informed decisions about how best to find fulfilment.

Flow

In *Finding Flow* by Mihaly Csikszentmihalyi,[61] the author writes:

> The metaphor of flow is one that many people have used to describe the sense of effortless action they feel in moments that stand out as the best in their lives. Athletes refer to it as 'being in the zone,' religious mystics as being in 'ecstasy,' artists and musicians as 'aesthetic rapture.'

In my coaching I ask, when do you feel, 'this is what I was born to do,' or when time just passes because you are so absorbed in something. In helping my clients identify those moments, it helps them in choosing to do more of the things that give them an experience of flow.

In the quote below, this full involvement is seen as of our own volition, not just circumstantial. It is something we choose to do, but in doing, gain joy.

> It is the full involvement of flow, rather than happiness, that makes for excellence in life. We can be happy experiencing the passive pleasure of a rested body, warm sunshine, or the contentment of a serene relationship, but this kind of happiness is dependent on favourable external circumstances. The happiness that follows flow is of our own making, and it leads to increasing complexity and growth in consciousness.'

In the following quote from *Flow* (58) we see the link between Csikszentmihalyi's theory of flow and the concepts of mastery and purpose. We are driven to achieve something we perceive as worthwhile and that requires effort. We are stretched and we grow, these experiences bring us happiness.

> The best moments occur when a person's body or mind is stretched to its limits in a voluntary effort to accomplish something difficult and worthwhile ... in the long run optimal experiences add up to a sense of mastery — or perhaps better, a sense of participation in determining the content of life — that comes as close to what is usually meant by happiness as anything else we can conceivably imagine." *Flow*. Mihaly Csikszentmihalyi 1990[62]

The Eight Characteristics of Flow

Csikszentmihalyi describes eight 'characteristics of flow':

1. We confront tasks we have a chance of completing;
2. We must be able to concentrate on what we are doing;
3. The task has clear goals;
4. The task provides immediate feedback;
5. One acts with deep, but effortless involvement, that removes from awareness the worries and frustrations of everyday life;
6. One exercises a sense of control over their actions;
7. Concern for the self disappears, yet, paradoxically the sense of self emerges stronger after the flow experience is over; and
8. The sense of duration of time is altered.

How To Find Flow

To find our place of flow, we must first understand ourselves and, in particular, identify our strengths. Describing experiences of life's joys brings into sharp focus those moments where the potential for flow is present. If we align the way we spend time, both in work and leisure, to a purpose we believe in, flow is more likely. Using our strengths and having a challenge that is just a little out of reach helps us to find flow, while understanding what feeds or what drains us helps us discover situations where we can operate in flow.

Tools

There are several tools that can assist in raising self-awareness regarding strengths. One is the work of The Gallup Organization, which conducted a systematic study of excellence by interviewing over a million people at the height of performance. This work informed the creation of StrengthsFinder, and was first published in Now *Discover Your Strengths* in 2001 by Markus Buckingham and Donald O Clifton Strengthfinder comprises 'thirty-four most prevalent themes of human talent' and provides a tool to identify a persons top five strengths

The StrengthsFinder tool is now also available online. Buckingham and Clifton propose that, counter to popular thought, the best opportunity for growth is to build on strengths rather than to address weaknesses. My experience of this tool is that it gives a language for people to discuss their strengths, raises self-awareness and affirms preferences.

There are other tools which also help, such as the Myers-Briggs Type Indicator® (MBTI®)[63] and, from ancient traditions, The Enneagram.[64]

IMPLICATIONS FOR CHRISTIANS IN CHURCH LEADERSHIP

How is success measured in church life? Counting church attendance and financial giving are the markers used to measure the success or decline of a church. I used to be Chair of Trustees for my church and during that time, these were the things we discussed at our meetings. I felt that what was often missed was the rich detail about the impact of the church in engaging members in furthering God's kingdom, both within the membership and in the wider community. I was also struck by how difficult it was to quantify the depth of the impact of transformation in individual lives.

In an interesting blog post, Pastor Carey Nieuwhof argues that church leaders need to focus first on engaging their members in mission, rather than on attendance.[65] He reminds us that Christians were called to 'follow' Jesus, not to 'attend'. It is the relationship people have with Jesus that draws them in; they are attracted to and engaged by Him and His gospel. Out of this comes engagement and involvement in mission, and the church is built from that.

I think there is a challenge for church leaders to involve people in meaningful ways. Much of our church culture is didactic, hierarchical and not easily accessible to millennial culture. Learning styles and expectations have changed; the internet and social media provide both challenges and huge opportunities to engage people in new ways. As mentioned before in this book, one of the fruits of the COVID-19 lockdown period was the rise of online church services and interactive ways to continue in community.

Earlier in this chapter, I explored definitions of engagement and one word struck me: connection. It is connection that deepens engagement and church leaders will need find ways to build those connections.

GOLDEN THREADS

SACRED PERSPECTIVES ON ENGAGEMENT

I often ask my clients to bring to mind times of joy: 'When have you experienced being who God created you to be?' Each person will have a different answer to that challenge because we are all unique – created as unique human beings, with our differences in strengths, preferences, traits and passions. However, we are all called to live out our primary calling to serve God and to use the strengths He has given us in that service. The Bible provides us with numerous examples of character strengths and with inspiring stories of how imperfect individuals used their strengths to further God's kingdom.

I love the teaching of Paul in both Ephesians and Corinthians. We are not all called to the same area of service: we are not all teachers, apostles, evangelists; we don't all have the same spiritual gifts. And in fact, I relish the gifts of others in church community.

I serve on a women's ministry team and we regularly put on events for women in our church. As a team, we are all different and this difference brings wonderful riches. We have those who are fantastic administrators, wise counsellors, researchers, enablers, visual creatives, and communicators. Between us we harness all these strengths to work towards a common goal, and experience the ease of working in community or team. None of us could accomplish the tasks on our own; we need each other. I believe this is how Jesus wants His Church to be: each individual, uniquely gifted, using their gifts for God's kingdom; each engaged in mission and called to a purpose.

Called To Be in Flow

My interest in coaching came from a deeply held belief that, when Jesus talked about fullness of life in John 10, He not only meant eternal life but a redeemed life whilst on earth. 'I have come that they may have life, and have it to the full' (John 10:10). For many reasons, life can rob us of that truth, so we need to reframe our thinking to accept it and find ways to live in fullness.

I developed Signposts Coaching to help clients find flow and fullness. Signposts Coaching[66] is a journey of discovery, which helps individuals find direction.

SIGNPOSTS COACHING PROCESS

My action research, based on work with clients, has led me to conclude that the following significant 'signposts' are needed to help someone find direction:

1. Self-acceptance and appreciation of unique qualities, strengths, joys and preferences.
2. Realistic appraisal of the current life context (constraints and enablers).
3. Having space to release and articulate dreams.
4. Having a vision for the future.
5. Exploring potential avenues and options.
6. Refining the vision.
7. Making a plan with goals and beginning to take steps towards them.

In sessions, using the metaphor of a simple pebble, we explore the concept of uniqueness. Just as each pebble is unique, hewn from a specific rock and shaped by tide and time, we are uniquely created, all of us in the image of God.

Psalm 139 gives a clear picture of God's perfect and intentional creation of us: 'For you created my inmost being... I praise you because I am fearfully and wonderfully made' (vv.13–14); 'All the days ordained for me were written in your book before one of them came to be' (v.16). In a culture of comparison, self-acceptance is a challenge for many. Aligning our view of self to a biblical perspective requires us to accept grace. As in the Cycle of Grace explored in Chapter 7, when we accept ourselves through the lens of God's acceptance, we are then motivated to act and to serve God.

Understanding the context of our lives requires us to put together a picture of all the parts, like a jigsaw, including strengths, dreams, moments of flow, qualifications, constraints and enablers, financial needs, geography, family and relationships. We need to have a full appreciation of all the factors that affect our lives to see ourselves more clearly – and we can trust that these factors are known to God, just as he promised Jeremiah: 'Before I formed you in the womb I knew you, and before you were born I consecrated you; I appointed you a prophet to the nations' (Jer. 1:5, AMP).

God also has plans for each one of us:

> For I know the plans I have for you, declares the LORD, plans for welfare and not for evil, to give you a future and a hope. Then you will call upon me and come and pray to me, and I will hear you. You will seek me and find me, when you seek me with all your heart. (Jeremiah 29:11–13, ESV)

We have to allow ourselves to dream and create a vision for our future before we can uncover the road ahead. Finding time and the creative space to imagine a better future and to allow our dreams to bubble up requires commitment. Some personalities find this easier than others; some see in landscape and others in fine details. The landscapers will refine the steps to the dream and the detailers will build up incrementally.

We often think that our dreams are not acceptable to God; but the Bible teaches that if we set our hearts on Him, delight in Him and seek His path, because He knows the desires of our hearts and He is a loving father, He will make our paths straight: 'Take delight in the LORD, and he will give you the desires of your heart' (Ps. 37:4–5); 'Commit to the LORD whatever you do, and he will establish your plans' (Prov. 16:3); 'In their hearts humans plan their course, but the LORD establishes their steps' (Prov. 16:9).

Signposts Coaching is aimed at helping others to find flow and to live in fullness. The principles I based it on and have included here may sound simple. Inevitably people need help exploring barriers, and the outworking of these principles in each life is often complex. But my experience of walking alongside others on this coaching journey has been a privilege, as I have seen people released from self-limiting beliefs, raise their aspirations, and find more fulfilling lives and much more flow.

ENGAGED BY JESUS

Jesus drew people to Him by the stories He told and by His ministry of miracles and healing. The transformation that caused the Christian Church to grow, from a group of followers who were frightened and in hiding after His death, to the courageous disciples who built the Church, was only possible through the Holy Spirit. God's power within them empowered and enabled courageous lives.

That same transformation is available to all of us, personally and for our organisations. It is my prayer that, through the work of the Holy Spirit and the ideas I have presented in Improving from WithIn, transformation will happen.

SECTION 3:
COLLECTIVE WISDOM FROM CHRISTIANS IN LEADERSHIP

Chapter 9
INTERVIEWS WITH CHRISTIANS IN LEADERSHIP

In October 2020, I met someone via Zoom who helped me shape this next section of the book. I was discussing my ideas about how leaders apply models and theory in practice; how they begin to lead change in practice; how they discern their priorities and the timing for interventions. This conversation built upon others I had been having about the complexities of leadership for those seeking to hold true to their Christian faith and to apply it in their work. I was curious about whether having a faith made the job of leading more complex and if some specific contexts were more difficult to navigate than others. As I discussed this with my Zoom companion, he said, 'Have you thought about interviewing leaders about this? I would love to read what they say.' At the time, I wasn't sure if this was the direction I wanted to pursue. But the idea settled with me and, as I began to form some questions, my excitement grew.

This chapter is dedicated to the 15 experienced Christian leaders who kindly gave me their time and were interviewed via Zoom. None will be named or directly acknowledged to preserve anonymity. I want to thank them for their honesty and the depth of reflection they shared with me. Spending time with these people has been a privilege and listening to the recordings to make my notes has been a joy. I can only hope that I can do justice to their wisdom in writing.

All the leaders I interviewed hold, or have retired from, senior leadership positions within the following settings: higher education, schools and education administration, churches, charities and governance, civil service, local government, National Health Service, business and consultancy. I asked them all the same questions but, as expected, our conversations took many different directions. The lens through which we view the world is shaped by our experience as well as our context. Most leaders had worked across different contexts and some, although working in a mainly secular setting, had also had experience of church leadership roles.

Our conversations covered the following themes:
- Diagnosis and getting started on the journey of change.
- Discerning the timing and pace for change.
- Making wise interventions.
- Inviting God into the process.
- Dealing with challenging and difficult issues.
- Working when key players are the issue.
- Power and the place for setting safe boundaries.
- Creating the climate.

I will endeavour to present the collective wisdom I heard in those conversations, framed around the questions I used in the interviews.

1. When you start the process of change, how do you go about diagnosing the issues and what do you draw on to inform you?

Listening and Observing

There was a consensus that listening is the first key to understanding what's going on in an organisation; time taken to do this thoroughly is invaluable. Seeking out the views of as many people as possible and from every level within, and sometimes outside, the organisation provides a depth of intelligence. Most of my interviewees were purposeful in instigating informal conversations with staff who had 'front line' roles, the fruit of these being the rich intelligence and breadth of perceptions of the current reality. This also demonstrated an intention to involve everyone in the process of change and encourage engagement at every level of the service.

One lovely example of this was a chief executive of a local authority, who encouraged front-line staff to give ideas and share examples of problems their service-users experience. At the start of the COVID-19 lockdown in 2020, the 12,000 vulnerable people in the area were identified and each one was contacted directly by a member of council staff. One staff member told the story of a recently widowed lady, living in a rural area, who relied upon her library for her wellbeing. The library had had to close, so it was decided that for her and for others in a similar position, a book delivery service would be established. This is an example of a listening, responsive and compassionate culture. No wonder the approval ratings for the way this council dealt with the pandemic were extremely high.

Listening, holding back opinions and paying attention were mentioned frequently. The ability to notice what's going on or to hear what 'stories' are being told, without asking questions or stepping in and offering opinions, gives leaders the opportunity to begin to form an impression of current strengths and challenges. One said, 'Listening to what is *not* said is as important as listening to what is articulated' (education leader). It can indicate there are 'no go' areas, or reasons for this that need enquiry or investigation.

Most of my interviewees described the technique of actively holding back to enable them to gain a deeper understanding before drawing their conclusions. There was broad consensus about the value of holding back, especially when new to the job: 'I listen "broadly" and hold myself back until I have a sense of the lines of enquiry I want to follow' (NHS senior manager). Once a leader begins to ask questions or give opinions, staff will often shape what they say to please the leader. This can skew the information that's shared. Remaining neutral for a short time, whilst explaining that you are trying to understand and get to know the organisation, and listen to staff, is helpful. But this has to be tempered with the need to give people a sense of who the leader is and what they expect. In my experience there is a balance to be struck when holding back, especially when people are looking for clues to establish whether they 'feel safe' with the new leader.

One leader described how she watches the ways people work together. Another described observing a team who didn't seem to be working well together; they lacked confidence in each other and were not achieving their outcomes. This was a clue that something was wrong and needed further investigation. He said, 'Although the knowledge is often held in the team, it can be difficult to access if there isn't transparency, or if people perceive they have something to lose if they talk about it' (retired director of education and trustee). He went on to describe how he'd invested time in trying to get to know how people 'ticked' and what motivated them, to build understanding and trust.

There was widespread agreement across my interviewees that

people within an organisation will know its strengths and weaknesses. If they are given the opportunity to share their thoughts during the diagnosis phase of change, they are more likely to 'buy in' when change begins.

Asking Good Questions and Using Language Skilfully

As well as listening, leaders asked well-formed questions. One described the process of waiting and observing, then gradually forming questions to tease out early thoughts of the core of the problem. Some described a growing sense of the core issues and asking questions to triangulate and investigate these thoughts and 'hunches'.

The use of language and how questions are phrased is important. One leader described how linguistic awareness can support in demonstrating contextual understanding, and build rapport. She suggested leaders should listen to the language being used and adopt phrases or reflect back those that are used within the organisation. She called this 'speaking the language'. This is particularly helpful when working across various disciplines, all of which have particular phrases that are understood within the discipline but may be nuanced differently elsewhere.

Open questions are helpful in keeping the agenda neutral and not steering the conversation. Avoid using questions that are leading or that will make the person feel defensive. Using questions that help people think more deeply or to expand on a thought is useful: 'You talked about x – that's interesting. Can you tell me a little more about that?'; or 'What you've said is really helpful. I wonder what evidence you've drawn on to make your conclusions.'

Another leader used feedback from others to encourage and elicit ideas from her staff. She described using the format, *they think, I think, I wonder what you think*, as a means to test out the evidence she was gathering.

I was particularly struck by one of my interviewees, a local council leader who has a deep belief in the capacity of his staff. He is committed to empowering his teams to find their own solutions to the challenges they face. He will often ask, 'What's stopping this happening?', then say, 'Let's find solutions to these problems.' This approach takes away the sense of blame if things are not working and encourages creative thinking.

In some cases, leaders used more formal questioning strategies, such as conducting organisational reviews, structured focus groups or staff surveys. These can be internally or externally facilitated. This strategy enables the collection of both quantitative and qualitative data and can often provide a confidential mechanism for people to share their views. I have used a variety of these methods frequently as a consultant. The power of this approach is particularly helpful when there is a level of denial of issues, or the leader needs additional evidence to strengthen the case for change.

One leader stated that this process of gathering rich data that informs and engages people in understanding the need for change needs to be owned by the whole organisation. He suggested that it should be an ongoing process, not just at the start of a new job, because it's easy to become familiar with the culture and assume you are reading the data, but miss important signals. For this reason, he uses his annual review and 360°-feedback tools for this. He said it was important for him to step back and review to stop himself becoming 'sucked in' to the status quo.

Another said she used tools such as SWOT analysis to understand, diagnose and help analyse. She also used case scenarios to demonstrate problems. These were presented as evidence and then she asked questions using the *they think, I think, I wonder what you think* format.

Data

Most of the leaders I interviewed had access to data sources. I found it interesting that each one had a preference for different types of data according to their particular strengths and professional backgrounds. The accountancy-trained sought out financial data; the linguists listened for clues from the language being used. The deeply relational leaders read the relationships and ways of working in teams. However, despite a preference for specific types of data, there was a consensus that data from several sources was invaluable in informing diagnosis. Using a number of sources to triangulate and inform further enquiry was recommended, and mixing hard numerical data with qualitative commentary was highly valued.

One concern was whether the data collected was the most helpful. In a church, for example, measuring financial giving or numbers attending on its own does not help to inform the level of real engagement, growth in discipleship or maturity of faith. This raises the question about what we choose to measure and collect data on. Similarly, in schools, exam data will not always tell the full story of the impact of the teacher and school community on the lives of its pupils.

Data and Governance

Several of my interviewees were involved in governance roles, either as directors, trustees or as school governors. Those in such significant roles, removed from the day-to-day leadership of an organisation, can experience challenges in accessing data. They are dependent upon the quality and accuracy of the data they are provided with. In situations where there are concerns about their organisations, they have to skilfully probe deeper and, in some cases, this requires them to become more hands-on than their role might normally permit.

One charity trustee expressed frustration at the data that was presented to the board. He'd realised that the levers available to them were insufficient and reflected that this is an added complexity and weighty responsibility to what is often a voluntary position of leadership. In this case, trustees would have to investigate more deeply, which requires becoming more hands-on than is normally considered appropriate.

The same person recommended conducting trustee-only meetings. This would allow them to ask the unthinkable questions and to gain a consensus as to how to proceed for the good of the organisation.

Diagnosis Jigsaw Pieces

What I found intriguing was the leaders who had access to wide data sets from a range of sources, but for whom this only provided a backdrop to their diagnosis. In a significant number of the interviews, people described the significance of observing the dissonance between the published position and actual practice: the drift from the core mission or stated values. One said he paid attention to 'the gap between what is written and what is actually going on' (NHS GP); another described this as the 'published but not lived' (headteacher).

Finding Drivers for Change

The gap between what is written and what is actually going on becomes one of the strongest drivers for change. Several of my interviewees spoke of the need to align practice with what is stated or published. We'll return to this when looking at the responses to climate creation.

Another common theme was the need to return to the vision, or mission and purpose, of the organisation, especially when there has been a drift away from this. The universality of the value placed on creating a common vision was particularly striking to me, as it resonates with my own work.

Digging Below the Waterline

The complexity of functioning below the waterline in the realm of ideas, beliefs and philosophies was of a frequent topic we discussed. One leader described the need to attend to the readiness of key stakeholders to accept ideas, or to assess the political will for a change. She talked about anticipating 'how it will land' before presenting her ideas. Another described endeavouring to understand and identify systemic beliefs or deeply held philosophical positions to help understand the cultural norms he was facing.

How leaders went about this was often described as 'paying attention' and using all available data to formulate a clear view of what change was needed. I was struck by the fact that, although there was widespread agreement with the need to listen, ask questions and use data, this toolkit was not complete without the willingness to have self-confidence in their intuitive or gut feelings about the situation.

2. How do you discern the timing for making an intervention?

My own experience has taught me that diagnosing what needs to change is often more straightforward than discerning the right time to make a change or begin an intervention. I was curious how my interviewees went about discerning the timing and what wisdom they might be willing to share about this. Their answers were illuminating, and I loved the mix of leadership wisdom and the humility of reliance on the spiritual disciplines of prayer and seeking wise counsel.

I'm going to share the golden nuggets I noted from each of my interviews.

I did a lot of prayer walking, reading scripture and listening for specific words that were backed up by scripture.

I endeavoured to understand the 'spiritual roots' of the organisation and of specific issues, such as pride, freemasonry, favouritism, that were present. In response, I began by adopting a servant leadership approach and sought to journey with people to find a way forward.

There is a growing sense in your spirit as you pay attention to others. A bit of daylight comes through or an insight you have been missing. The next piece of the jigsaw puzzle.

You pick up on the external environment and this prompts you to make changes internally in response (for example, new legislation, funding, demand for new courses).

Higher education

I pray about it and trust my intuition. I rely upon the wisdom of words and key conversations to shape my thinking.

Timing often comes from personal prayer, sitting and thinking through what's going on. It's both mind and heart, brain wisdom, intuition and timely conversations. A holistic 360-degree listening; practice, experience and intuition with head, heart and intuition connecting.

Wait for the rest of the team to be ready or to have seen it themselves. Use external review to affirm and confirm.

Educator, coach and facilitator

Be wise with timing; hold back and play the long game if needed. For example, if someone is about to retire, there's no need to hasten their exit. If people are tired, change can overload them. Don't bring in things at the wrong time of the term.

Sometimes the right time won't come and people will try to block change, or it will be unpopular with staff, but don't procrastinate.

I listen to God, pray about it and how it feels. If it feels wrong, then I won't do it. I talk to other Christians whose opinions I value.

Headteacher

Timing of organisational development is a process not a one-off. Days away can help facilitate it; ongoing incremental change; building gradually a good structure. I knew what I wanted and we went for it.

I aimed to align how an organisation should look with theology, and set up an approach based on Christian values. I see Christian values sitting well in a secular organisation.

NHS commissioner and GP

I live in the tension between my own vision, sense of opportunity, creativity and imagination and desire to be in the future – and the ability to be still and wait. To be at peace and to wait and be thankful for what is.

It's His work and I am there as His steward of something that doesn't belong to me, but at the same time I passionately own it.

Collective discernment is needed and to build it we need our own personal spiritual disciplines to be strengthened. We paid more attention to our internal spiritual life with daily morning routines.

Higher education mission

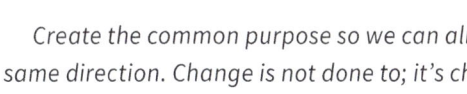

Create the common purpose so we can all move together in the same direction. Change is not done to; it's change together.

Emergency planning for the first lockdown on 23 March 2020 and I felt all at sea. Where was my inspiration? Reading Acts daily and St Paul's letters enabled me to tap into spiritual wisdom.

We had to change the world for a lot of people. I had a sense of burden for these people. What could we do? How could we start championing the health and wellbeing of those people? I had a pastoral concern. How could we journey together through this?

Council leader

Prayer and prayer support from others. It's not a magic bullet – you have to seek to get it right. Prayerful wisdom to read the times is more important than specific timing. You need to know and understand the times you are in.

Timing one's interventions is an art not a science and it requires prayer for wisdom.

Trustee

Spend time helping people to see what needs to change so all are on the same page. Help people get to the same conclusions and see the dissatisfaction with where we are. Then they will ask, 'How do we get there? We can't stay here.'

Colossians 4:2 says, 'Devote yourselves to prayer, being watchful and thankful' – watchful to what's going on around, knowing the times and trying to see things as God sees them. What does He think of this? Does it break His heart?

Devotion to prayer is a habit and, for ongoing decision-making, it's a life habit; part of who I am and part of life.

Timing: we got a very clear moment when financial data meant we had to make tough decisions. We had to make the call or we couldn't achieve the mission.

Mission leader and trustee

Learning to take it slower and realise that I need to be comfortable with leaving things and not rushing in. I don't have to do everything or to achieve as we have a core purpose and our strategy towards it.

We are committed to serve in the direction we are guided in, living out 'thy kingdom come'.

For collective discernment, we meet every morning for prayer on Zoom and, through the practice of daily Bible reading, God speaks to us each day.

Church of England education

I am invited in to help, usually because of my connections. I hold up the mirror and help them understand. I worked with the trustee board and provoked the change.

God is orderly and uses process to try to find a third way, moving through love and courage. God provides a compass, not a map, you have to look for mystery, have humility, and practice double listening to listen to the prophetic. Get both in the room.

Retired civil servant now consultant

It's easier in a secular business to make a change. In Christian settings, often there is 'founder syndrome' – people hold on to things that they perceive the founder would do.

I couldn't make the changes I wanted and had to walk away and let someone else pick it up to do the next bit. God has moved the mountains and what needed to happen has happened. God's timing not our timing.

In another situation, I bided my time and waited until key people had retired before making the change, out of respect for previous leaders. I sense when isn't the right moment and check in my spirit when I shouldn't do something.

Leadership coach and interim CEO

I look for total unity and then move on it. Timing is not normally an issue.

Church Leader

Led by the Holy Spirit for wisdom, pray on things. Look for confirmation in each spirit if something is right.

Church Leader

Through team, you might get a part of it but rare to get the whole thing. God speaks to another member and another brings a piece too. Shared listening is helpful and safer.

Strong hunches are tested out with others and my Spiritual Director. If I feel it's not taking hold or there's a piece missing, then I think we've got it wrong.

Church leader

Since I've been working from home, it's been easier to stop and pray, living openly in the Spirit of God and listening. There's a quality to my relationship with God; a centred place. It happens when I'm connected to God. I get hunches about things. I'm self-aware, I listen to myself, I believe God is in me. I am called to this role at this time, and I am delighted to be in His hands, in this place, at this time.

NHS Commissioner

My reflections on these conversations were that each of these people had drawn on the strength of their personal spiritual discipline of prayer; had found wisdom in seeking the wise counsel of others; had sought to understand the timing, both contextually and intuitively; and had woven all these together to help them move forward. I was struck by the fact that this was true for those in both secular and Christian settings, and that all recognised that, when it comes to timing, it's in God's hands.

Our conversations broadened into exploring how they invited God into the process of leading change. The overwhelming response was personal prayer and their own spiritual disciplines. I was also impressed by the strength of belief that leadership was a calling for which they had been equipped by God. They were to use the strengths and gifts He had given them for the benefit of the organisation within which they worked.

This quote powerfully makes that point.

> *Since I have been working from home it's been easier to stop and pray. Living in an open spirit to God, listening. Quality of my relationship with God. Centred place. Happens when I am connected to God. I get hunches about things. I am self aware, I listen to myself, believe God is in me. I am called to this role at this time, I am delighted to be his hands, in this place, at this time.*
>
> NHS Commissioner

3. What are the most challenging or difficult issues you face?

I was curious about the greatest challenges or most difficult issues faced by leaders. Was it different when working in secular or Christian settings?

Dealing With People

The number one area of concern was dealing with people and the interpersonal and relational challenges that are raised when working with others. This was the same for all settings but there was agreement that in some Christian organisations, where HR systems were less developed or there was a strong culture of 'family', the complexity of navigating relationships was particularly challenging. This was seen most frequently in the church context.

One described the impact of a particular individual's ego and use of power in creating resistance to moving an organisation forward. Another spoke of a power struggle between team members who clashed and actively disliked each other. One described feeling that people could become opaque and not able to identify what's going on internally or the particular values or beliefs at play. These experiences are not unique to leaders who have a Christian faith, and mirror those I have come across over the years, either myself or in dialogue with the leaders I have worked with.

Understanding the motivations that sit below the surface of an individual, or create 'group think', helps to provide clues to how a leader may explore these issues. Having a language to explore differences in personality types is also helpful. If a team have a mutual understanding of tools such as Myers-Briggs or StrengthsFinder, then they can develop a shared language to explore difference and to begin to appreciate the strengths a diversity of perspectives brings to the team.

I asked what helped leaders navigate the complexities of these situations. Effective and courageous communication was the key: having conversations to bring these underlying things into the open seemed to be the solution, albeit not easy to achieve. There was a consensus that these issues needed to be confronted and, in doing so, the potential for them to become toxic was lessened.

Doing the Right Thing

Some of my conversations focused on the pain of doing the right thing when it had a negative impact on others or would be unpopular. To do this, even when there was a cost, was perceived as a requirement of the job as a leader but one which needed courage. One commented that he had to focus on the bigger purpose of the organisation and that, even though to move forward was painful, that pain was more bearable because he knew the organisation and its mission would benefit in the long run. This point was made by others too, who cautioned against procrastination or giving people false hope by avoiding the inevitable need for staffing changes.

Addressing underperformance or disciplinary personnel issues posed high levels of stress to most leaders. This was across all contexts. There was agreement that in situations where established and effective HR systems and processes were in place, this was helpful. People commented that churches often did not have these systems and, as a result, such situations when they arose in church communities were particularly complex to navigate. This was attributed to the 'family' or relational nature of church, and in some cases a reluctance to adopt best practice from 'the world' – or, as one recalled it being expressed: 'We don't want your worldly business ways here'.

The Identity of the Leader

One intriguing area we explored was the impact that being a leader had on the person's own identity. A number commented that they had been reluctant to see themselves as leaders but realised that other people viewed them differently because of their role or the status that came with it. This brought with it the realisation that with responsibility came the need to undertake the role with integrity. One commented that he had been surprised by leadership, initially taking quite a passive approach to it, but he'd realised he needed to be courageous and begin to shake things up.

Another reflected on the realisation that he had the power to make things happen. Initially, he'd denied he had power and he was afraid of that power. He had to learn to accept it and use it. We'll return to the theme of power again later in this chapter when I explore safe power boundaries.

A couple of conversations focused on how to invest in the role of leader and to take ownership of it to make an impact, while maintaining a safe boundary between your role and your own identity.

One church leader said, 'When it's going well, you think it's about you, and when it goes wrong, it's about you and your identity – being servant-hearted and not in love with the role. Don't put your identity into the role.' Recalling the quote I used earlier from a higher education mission leader – 'It's His work and I'm there as His steward of something that doesn't belong to me, but at the same time I passionately own it' – there's a real balance to be struck in keeping these two in tension. It's one that requires strength of character and self-awareness.

A common theme discussed was that, when things begin to go wrong in leadership, it's often because the leader's own identity is being threatened. As a result, they self-protect to ensure their personal identity is secure. In the scenarios we discussed where this has occurred, there was agreement that it usually came about when there was a perceived threat to the leader's predominant driver, often that of power.

Power in Leadership

The theme of power was a feature of all my conversations. We discussed the power of key players, the need for creating safe boundaries and the potential for abuse of power.

We talked about how key players might hold power irrespective of status or position. The impact they could have in blocking change or in exerting pressure and influence were seen as a potential problem for leaders. Some examples of this were of trustees or governors exerting undue pressure or operating outside the formal structures and processes to canvass opinion.

In some cases, the influence came from key players who were no longer part of the organisation, especially if they had founded it initially. Several of my interviewees talked of 'founder syndrome' (previously mentioned), where the perception of what the founder would do hung heavily in the air. In one case, the founder had long since died, but the organisation was wedded to continuing as that person would have wanted. The difficulty here was that the founder had been entrepreneurial while the successors were more conservative in style. The perception of what the founder might do now was holding the organisation back, the irony being that, had they still been there, they would have been much more likely to instigate change.

Another aspect of power discussed was how to create safe boundaries around it so as not to abuse the position of power. A doctor, who has tussled with these themes, described how his practice has changed over the years and has been influenced by learning from an organisation which supports abused women. He described his experience of training in medical school, which was predominantly male-led, authoritative and with a culture of telling people what to do. Having immersed himself in the literature of abuse, he has adopted a different way of working with his patients. He now works hard to 'partner with' them rather than to be directive.

One person said, 'We need to understand power and the advantages it gives us.' This means being conscious of the power the position affords and being particularly aware of the situations where we could directly affect other people's lives. One described how he attempted to 'walk in their shoes' for a while when considering how his decisions affected others. He tried to scrutinise his own power by being honest with himself, and allowed close colleagues to speak into situations and provide a check and balance.

When leaders had to restructure or make staffing changes, there was consensus on the need to follow best practice in human resources and use legal processes with integrity. This was also seen as a potential area where clear boundaries needed to be set, so that pastoral support was not muddled with official procedures. Again, this was particularly complex within Christian organisations, where prayer and pastoral support are practised as a norm. One example of this was a leader who refused to allow an employee's request for flexible working. Having issued a formal letter, the leader then offered to pray for the person. The employee felt this placed them in a position where the decision was perceived as having God's blessing, and believed the leader was using prayer as a means of justifying their decision, which was inappropriate. Another leader described the need to separate their role as CEO and that of pastor. He only prayed with employees at their request. By taking the lead from them, it provided the safer boundary for prayer.

One trustee has recently undertaken a review of safeguarding for his organisation and become more aware of issues of white privilege, race and of the potential for institutional and spiritual abuse. He felt these issues were not being addressed fully enough by the Christian community and that the way we interpret the Bible is sometimes used to justify behaviour that is inappropriate.

God Said

Christians are not immune from using the 'God trump card', and there was universal concern over phrases like 'God said' or 'I heard God say' when putting a position across. This becomes problematic when used to wield power or to justify an entrenched position. How can you disagree with such statements and what if you think God is telling you something else? In conflict situations, where both parties think they are hearing from God, this can compound polarisation.

For church leaders especially, whose job it is to discern what God might be saying, this is particularly tricky. Those I talked to agreed that seeking the wisdom of others to confirm or challenge what they were discerning provides a valuable safety net. Using language thoughtfully can also help engender a spirit of humility: *I am sensing… What do you think…? What are you hearing…?* Allowing others to challenge, input, add to and affirm are all healthy practices for leaders.

One leader struggling with a conflict situation in his church talked of sleepless nights, as there seemed to be no way forward to bring about unity in his church leadership team. Individuals, he thought, had become entrenched and polarised, both camps believing they knew what God was saying. He drew wisdom from biblical leaders who had learned to work together, and from teaching on unity and reconciliation.

This same leader felt that the church, in seeking forgiveness and looking for grace, could sometimes fail to act decisively when hard decisions needed to be made: 'Sometimes I feel we err on the side of grace and we actually should not let things go.'

As Christians, we endeavour to discern and hear from God and to be guided by biblical teaching. As Christians in positions of leadership, we need to find ways to do this that enable us to be sensitive to the Holy Spirit and remain centred in God, whilst also being able to discern when we might have got it wrong or are using God as a means to justify our own will.

Serving in Secular Workplaces

Those who worked in secular organisations, all of whom believed they had been called to their leadership roles and saw their work as service or ministry, faced other challenges.

How openly 'Christian' should they be? Was disclosing the root of their personal values helpful or acceptable to others? How should they talk about their faith with colleagues? One doctor described how he offered Christian values when developing a new NHS organisation. He felt they had been widely welcomed and that 'Christian values sit well in a secular organisation'.

Frequently, the leaders I spoke with described how their behaviours were shaped by their faith: 'It is just who I am,' said one. When serving in secular contexts, leaders did not necessarily see the need to be overt about their faith, but they did see the need to have integrity and be true to their beliefs.

Those working in health, education and other front line services felt a growing appreciation of their work as the dispersed church, being salt and light or 'His hands, in this place, at this time'.

4. How do you go about creating the culture that reflects your beliefs?

The final area we explored during the interviews was climate and culture. As this is such a significant aspect of my model, I wanted to know in practice what leaders did to create a culture that reflected their beliefs. I found that many of the conversations focused on climate or culture before I had even asked the question. It was clear to me that this is seen as a fundamental aspect of leadership and that there was a high degree of understanding about the impact it has on creating effective organisations.

My first interviewee had worked in a range of different higher education institutions and was now working within one that required a significant shift in practice. This is what he said:

> *I got stuck in and then people came along with me. Show people the journey so far and remind them of the successes. Incremental steps show there really is a need to change. You have to trust people and create a no-blame culture.*

Another commented on the value of story.

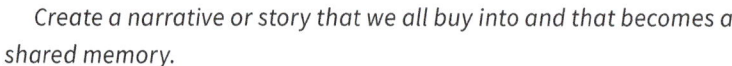

> *Create a narrative or story that we all buy into and that becomes a shared memory.*

This leader also reflected on the impact that too much change had on culture and where change is used to wield power. She believed that choosing values that supported people, and practising listening and checking in as supportive measures maintained the collective ability to thrive.

An experienced headteacher remarked that there was no agreed way to measure culture, but that it was created by living held values outwardly. The challenge was to remove the difference between the public and private; to be consistent. In a school, he thought that the headteacher was the key player in creating the culture.

> *The person at the top of the organisation shapes culture. You are the key driver. Do it as soon as you arrive to establish culture.*
> *Its ephemeral and intangible.*

A doctor in general practice recognised the importance of culture.

> *Culture is the most significant thing in any organisation. What you say and what you do.*
> *You need to understand what is published but not lived – discover the reality and not just what is written. Are people living and breathing it? Is there dissonance between what is declared and what is happening? Involve people throughout. It's about aligning. It comes from the top.*

One conversation concluded that culture is changed by behaviour: by choosing the behaviours you want and which will align to the values, you can establish the culture. This leader commented that inconsistent behaviours do damage. In his organisation, this means seeking to be collective followers of Christ.

> *Building patterns of behaviour that reflect what it means to be a follower of Christ. Lived behaviour and habitus.*

I had one conversation with a leader currently working in NHS commissioning, who works across different professional disciplines, all of which have slightly different cultures. She felt that her best contribution was to keep working at the relationships and continually model trust by being trustworthy. This meant doing what she said she would do. She also thought that, by being honest and sometimes making herself vulnerable by admitting she didn't always understand, and that not understanding was OK, this helped her to build trust across these boundaries.

A council leader described how his practice was influenced by neuroscience and how to create positive mindsets. He felt that mindsets are created by conversations and the language that is used: 'What can we achieve?'; 'What is going to help us crack this challenge?'; 'What are the values that are attractive and positive that give us that sense of purpose?' He also thought it was important to create a culture of success, so he encouraged people to tell their stories of success to model that culture.

A leader working in mission saw the link between vision, values, behaviour and climate. This meant that difficult conversations were required.

> *You need to establish the climate and have difficult conversations when character and behaviours are not aligned to the vision and values. Behaviours build climate.*

He believed the whole culture needed to be developed with all staff, recognising the cultural legacy from the past. This would set clear foundations for the future.

A retired civil servant, who had worked successfully in bringing about cultural change in her department, spoke of the need to change beliefs in order to change perceptions and culture. We discussed the process she had used to do this.

> *How did we change beliefs? We used value words and discussed them every Monday morning, earthing them in reality: what does it mean to you? So we reinforced the same language and behaviours.*

She recognised that different behaviours could come from the same values and said that she had had to open up conversations to challenge thinking and keep a dialogue going. This process had taken time but had become embedded.

I will conclude with her wise words.

> *Hold your nerve and have the courage to break the mould.*

SECTION 4:
FINDING GOLD – A CALL FOR RESTORATION

Chapter 10
LETTER TO TODAY'S NEHEMIAHS

LESSONS ON RESTORATION AND HOPE

What are the challenges facing leaders now? The world continues to feel unstable; economic hardship, political volatility and climate change are constant threats. We are struggling to deal with the global impact of numerous crises and humanitarian challenges that seem beyond our capacity to solve. The constant flow of negative news feeds creates fear and, with it, despair. Many are weary and struggling to find the energy to rise to the challenges ahead.

How do leaders respond and lead in these times? What have we learned from our collective experience and the shared trauma of a pandemic, and what is our response to continued uncertainty? As with all significant events, there are positive changes and innovations that will shape our future. How do we embrace these and build on them? Are we ready to assess the task of rebuilding or reshaping to address the many issues we now face? Is there a heightened awareness of pre-existing issues that need addressing or an urgency to respond differently to the needs of clients and communities?

As a leader, how you steer your people through such times will require wisdom, compassion and the restorative breath of the Holy Spirit.

I have been reflecting on the focus for this chapter and return to the story of Nehemiah, who heard of the desolation of the walls of Jerusalem and, responding to God's call, set off to rebuild them. Much has been written of Nehemiah's leadership and I do not wish to add to that. However, I think Nehemiah teaches us also of God's heart for restoration and the hope that restoration brings. It is this I want to explore in this chapter.

God's heart for restoration is central to His plan for reversing the breaking of relationship with Adam in the sacrifice of Jesus. Thus He enables a restoration of relationship between Himself and humankind for those who choose to accept it. Restoration (or the word 'restore') appears multiple times in the Bible, and the concept of restoration is at the heart of many stories and psalms.

One beautiful passage that speaks powerfully of this is Isaiah 61. Here we read of a reversal of brokenness or desolation, which is replaced by something more beautiful. This speaks of God's heart and His tenderness towards the broken, those who mourn and those who are in difficult circumstances. As a promise for this uncertain season, I find it uplifting and inspiring.

> The Spirit of the Sovereign LORD is on me,
> because the LORD has anointed me
> to proclaim good news to the poor.
> He has sent me to bind up the broken-hearted,
> to proclaim freedom for the captives
> and release from darkness for the prisoners,
> to proclaim the year of the LORD's favour
> and the day of vengeance of our God,
> to comfort all who mourn,
> and provide for those who grieve in Zion –
> to bestow on them a crown of beauty
> instead of ashes,
> the oil of joy
> instead of mourning,
> and a garment of praise
> instead of a spirit of despair.
>
> They will be called oaks of righteousness,
> a planting of the LORD
> for the display of his splendour.
> They will rebuild the ancient ruins
> and restore the places long devastated;
> they will renew the ruined cities
> that have been devastated for generations.
> Strangers will shepherd your flocks;
> foreigners will work your fields and vineyards.
> And you will be called priests of the LORD,
> you will be named ministers of our God.

You will feed on the wealth of nations,
and in their riches you will boast.

Instead of your shame
you will receive a double portion,
and instead of disgrace
you will rejoice in your inheritance.
And so you will inherit a double portion in your land,
and everlasting joy will be yours.

'For I, the LORD, love justice;
I hate robbery and wrongdoing.
In my faithfulness I will reward my people
and make an everlasting covenant with them.
Their descendants will be known among the nations
and their offspring among the peoples.
All who see them will acknowledge
that they are a people the LORD has blessed.'

I delight greatly in the LORD;
my soul rejoices in my God.
For he has clothed me with garments of salvation
and arrayed me in a robe of his righteousness,
as a bridegroom adorns his head like a priest,
and as a bride adorns herself with her jewels.
For as the soil makes the young plant come up
and a garden causes seeds to grow,
so the Sovereign LORD will make righteousness
and praise spring up before all nations. (Isaiah 61)

I believe there is a call on those in leadership to be part of the restoration story for this current season; to be God's hands and feet in bringing about the exchange of the spirit of despair so as to build oaks of righteousness; to bring the hope of God's kingdom and of Jesus with us in these days.

Another image that has been very powerful for me in recent months is the Japanese art of Kintsugi.

In Kintsugi, broken pots are mended with seams of gold, creating not only a restored and useful pot, but also a more beautiful object than its previous iteration. I have frequently been drawn back to this concept and imagery as I ponder the heart of restoration. I believe this too speaks into this season: we long to see things and people restored but also for something more beautiful and of greater value to replace what has gone before. There is a natural heart cry to go back to what was, but an even stronger one to rebuild in new and better ways in future.

Meditating on the theme of gold – first in the early chapters of this book as I unpacked the golden threads that have informed and guided my thinking, and now with the concept of seams of gold in the process of restoration and rebuilding – my prayer is that, as leaders, you will each find the seams of gold that can bring life in all its fullness to those you serve.

However, before we can move on to restoration, we need to pause and take stock of where we are currently.

Assessing the Task Ahead

I return to Nehemiah. In chapter 2, he privately inspects the walls of Jerusalem to see the extent of the devastation. Once he understands it, he then outlines the problem to others and calls them to rebuild. There is something in the wisdom of Nehemiah in assessing and understanding before calling others to the task ahead. As leaders, is there a need to step back and assess before taking any steps forward? How well do you understand the impact of, for example, a collective trauma such as the global pandemic? How has it played out for your organisation and the staff within it?

How do you facilitate a conversation to surface the hidden impact and diversity of responses individuals may be experiencing?

One model that may be helpful in providing wisdom here closely resembles the Kubler-Ross Cycle of Grief and is based on the work of Zunin and Myers in 1990.[67] Their model, Phases of Collective Trauma, provides an insight into possible responses and timeline for recovery and rebuilding. The model below has been adapted to reflect the pandemic crisis of the early 2020s (Washington State House Democrats).

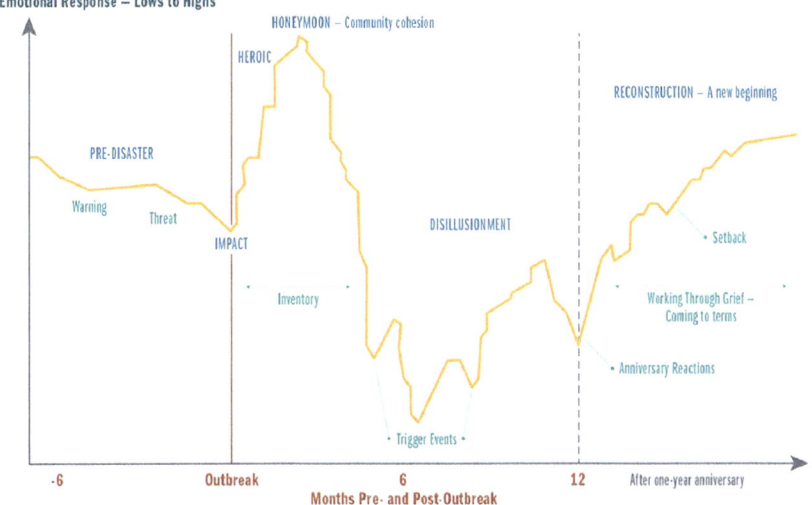

In the different phases of disaster, people experience a range of emotions and responses. Through the early stages, there is often a heroic response, acts of selflessness and an appreciation of those who step up to respond. This is accompanied by a rush of adrenalin that drives people to respond to the urgency of the situation, followed by the honeymoon where communities pull together to act. In the early months of COVID-19, we saw this in the regular 'clap for carers' and volunteering.

As time passes, there is a natural 'inventory' or reality period, when people realise their limits and understand the impact of the disaster. This is also the start of the disillusionment phase during which people begin to experience both physical and emotional weariness. Feelings of grief and anxiety as well as lethargy and helplessness can occur. During this time there may be specific trigger events, such as anniversaries, that compound the sense of grief.

Eventually we move to the reconstruction phase, when there are new beginnings and a new normal is created. This process is often bumpy with setbacks; people need to be able to work through their grief, to lament and to come to terms with what has been lost. As they do, both awareness of loss and hope for the future can coexist. It is now that people can move forward to restore and rebuild. This is sometimes referred to as the 'wiser living phase', during which there is an acknowledgement that what has occurred has changed the community in lasting ways. Healing can happen but there will be scars and wounds that continue.

This model reflects the Kubler-Ross Cycle of Grief but seeks to explain a collective or community experience that comes about by *everyone* experiencing a disaster. It doesn't assume that everyone will go through the same emotions at the same time, and we need to acknowledge that everyone's experience of a disaster will be different. Our own journey through the phases will be marked by our personal experiences and those of the people immediately around us.

As leaders, it is helpful for you to understand the individual journeys of your team and to find ways to support the grief process. It may be helpful to use the model above to explore where people feel they are currently. This will help you assess if they ready to rebuild or if there is a need to hold back on new initiatives until people are set to move forward, facilitating a wider conversation with your teams to discover what the prevailing phase is for the majority in your organisation.

Discovering Your Seam of Gold?

Let us consider the Kintsugi metaphor again: if your pot has been cracked or broken, where are the fracture lines? What would it look like to mend these so that you create something that is more beautiful and effective, and reflects the wisdom that is more precious than gold?

For many leaders there has been a realisation that the need to invest in human flourishing, often expressed as wellbeing, is the greatest challenge ahead. As well as the systemic and economic cost of the COVID-19 pandemic, the human cost in individual lives, mental health and recovery from trauma will need to be addressed. Human flourishing is at the heart of the gospel message. Jesus came to bring life in fullness – is this the time to consider how you can bring fullness of life to others through your work?

Trauma in General

The model can be applied to various experiences of collective trauma as they affect an organisation or community. The stages and processes are the same and leaders who understand these patterns will be able to identify strategies that support their people through them. My experience of working with groups of people who have all experienced the same trauma/s has been that, the more frequent the occurrence that precipitates the trauma, the more prolonged the felt impact is. When a group experiences a number of traumas in succession, the more resistant they are to recovery. If your organisation has been through a tumultuous period of multiple traumatic events, your people will be weary and wary of further change. Leaders will need to rebuild trust and demonstrate a consistency of restorative behaviours and actions. These encourage people to hope in a better future again.

Finding Hope

Hope provides the energy to combat weariness and despair. It draws people onwards towards that better future and provides the motivation for them to join together in creating it. Hope is the light shining through the clouds on a dark day, reminding us that, even when we can't see the sun, it is always there; hope is the gentle nudge of Emmanuel, God with us. The same image is often used to illustrate the thin place, where heaven touches earth. As leaders, how can we help others to see this light and find the energy of hope?

APPLICATION OF IMPROVING FROM WITHIN IN RESTORATION

Using Improving from WithIn Dimensions To Support Restoration with Gold

As a leader, you will need to find clarity for the way ahead. This may feel difficult in such uncertain times. Improving from WithIn Dimensions can provide a framework you can use to establish where you might need to focus your attention. As a coach, I have found that questions are most helpful in guiding and challenging thinking. I offer the following to assist in this process.

IMPROVING FROM WITHIN FOUNDATION DIMENSIONS

Alignment
- What could restoration with seams of gold look like for you and your organisation?
- Is this the time to revisit your mission or core purpose?
- Did the pandemic challenge the reason your organisation exists?
- Is there a greater urgency to achieve your mission?
- How well have your values been expressed?
- Are there new values you need to incorporate to better protect human flourishing and wellbeing?
- What vision do you have for the next season?
- How evident is hope as expressed through your leadership?
- What practices need to be embedded now?
- Are there lessons you have learned collectively that can inform future practice?

Climate Creation
- How does it feel in your organisation?
- Are there any fracture lines and, if so, how can they be restored?
- Where are people collectively and individually with regard to trauma recovery?
- How can you support people through the process of recovery?
- What consistent leadership behaviours do people need to see to bring greater flourishing?
- Have there been any challenges to the existing culture (positive or negative) that need addressing?

Leading Change
- Leading for human flourishing; leading with love at the heart; what do these mean for you?
- Is your organisation ready for change?
- How certain are you of the direction you want to set?
- What are the changes you want to see to achieve your vision for this next season?
- Does your staffing structure meet the needs of the vision?
- What leadership challenges do you face when leading through uncertainty?
- What support have you in place to help you?

OUTCOME DIMENSIONS

Innovation
- What positive and innovative ideas have emerged during the past couple of years?
- How can you harness these for good going forward?
- Where is the energy for innovation to meet new challenges ahead?
- How can you facilitate your people in their creative thinking?
- What is getting in the way of innovation and creativity?
- How can you remove these barriers?
- Where would collaboration with others assist in building a more creative culture and encourage innovation?

Motivation
- What leadership style do you need to harness to maximise the motivation of your people?
- Has trust grown in your organisation due to different working practices?
- Is there more autonomy for individual staff to decide how and when to deliver their work?
- How does your leadership style impact on others' journey through trauma recovery?
- How well do senior leaders understand the impact of trauma on energy levels, and what collective processes need to take place to support people to move forwards?
- How can you encourage and release intrinsic motivation?

Engagement
- How well are you engaging your people in conversations about their experiences, ideas and learning?
- How can you engage people in moving forwards?
- What new practices do you want to establish to encourage engagement and flourishing?
- How do you capture the learning and growth that people have experienced so you can collectively benefit from its wisdom?

SECTION 5:

DIAGNOSTIC CHECKLIST TOOL

Chapter 11
DIAGNOSTIC CHECKLIST: IMPROVING FROM WITHIN

FINDING WHERE TO START

Throughout this text, I've mentioned the use of diagnostics to help establish the starting point for any intervention. In 2012, I worked with a colleague to develop some diagnostic questions to help pinpoint where to focus when using the Improving from WithIn model.

We began by identifying the features you would see in a thriving organisation where intrinsic motivation was evident and people were flourishing. We took each of the model dimensions and overlaid the three concepts of autonomy, mastery and purpose from Dan Pink's work. From this, we arrived at a diagnostic checklist comprising of 18 key questions. We then created an additional set of questions focused on an individual's personal response to working in an organisation.

Initially, we put these online using Survey Monkey, believing this to be a helpful tool for organisations to survey staff and present data. However, I have also used the questions in focus groups to aid discussion.

In offering the Improving From WithIn Diagnostic, I have had to wrestle with a dilemma: do I place it behind a paywall on an online platform, which would enable those using it to present data and analyse the results? This would also ensure the work is protected and not misinterpreted. Or do I simply offer the reader the questions and trust them to use the Diagnostic with care, not abusing the gift of it by using it for financial gain, or by presenting it without acknowledging the source?

In the end, my conclusion has been that Improving from WithIn was given to me by God to steward so others could use it. For this reason, I feel I am to simply pass that gift on. So please use the questions with care, reference the source and do not breach copyright.

GOLDEN THREADS

IMPROVING FROM WITHIN

Diagnostic Questions

These questions can be used in questionnaires or as discussion questions with individuals or groups.

If choosing to use as a staff questionnaire, it is helpful to distinguish the respondent's role and length of service. This is because sometimes in an organisation, a range of perceptions exist at different levels within it. Length of service can provide helpful insight when respondents have experienced specific events, as these can affect their views. (Consider potential confidentiality issues when asking individuals to provide this information.)

It is helpful to explain why you are conducting the questionnaire/conversation and the reason your organisation is exploring this approach. For example:

'The purpose of these questions is to establish to what extent the features of thriving and self-sustaining improvement already exist in our (school/church/organisation). We want to understand how it feels to work here and to find out if there are specific things we can do to help us to continue to thrive and address things that could be improved.'

These questions are based around the Improving from WithIn model, comprised of six dimensions. Each dimension has short descriptors of what we would expect to see in an organisation that is thriving and has a culture of self-sustaining improvement.

Dimensions of the Improving from WithIn Model

Alignment
This is the process of alignment between the core mission (or purpose) of an organisation – its vision, the values it promotes – and actual practice.

Climate Creation
The climate is secured by unrelenting attention to secure consistent behaviours that promote the underpinning beliefs and agreed values;

these behaviours become 'the way we do things around here' and, when adopted by the whole community, create a secure ethos.

Leading Change
Leading change requires effective leadership behaviours, strategies and skills; it also requires an understanding of positive psychology and an appreciation of human flourishing and motivation to ensure that all adopt new behaviours and are empowered and take ownership of change.

Improvement and Innovation
Improvement, when truly effective, arises out of a desire to make things better, to solve problems or to master new skills. It is a creative process which needs to be owned by the members of an organisation. It's often a cycle that requires experimentation, trial and error, revision and refining. At its best, this creative process will invite innovation.

Motivation
In order for human beings to thrive and to perform at their best, they need to be motivated. Extrinsic (external) drivers are far less motivating than intrinsic(from within a person) ones. Organisations able to harness and encourage intrinsic motivation will outperform the rest.

Engagement
When human beings are motivated, they become engaged; when they are engaged, deep learning and high performance take place. In such organisations a climate of meaningful purpose develops, along with behaviours associated with 'going the extra mile' and generosity of spirit.

QUESTIONS

1. What is your role?
2. How long have you worked here?

SECTION A

This section is about how people perceive the organisation.
Please score the following descriptors.
4= true 3=mostly true 2=partially true 1=not true

Alignment	4	3	2	1
1. We trust each other to align practice to the mission, vision and values				
2. Our mission, vision and values are aspirational and guide our practice				
3. We have a clarity of purpose which enables us to achieve our vision and demonstrate our values				
Climate Creation				
4. We are all committed to behaving in ways that are consistent with the vision and values				
5. We have an inspirational core purpose that is reflected in our practices and behaviours				
6. We commit to improving the way we do things so we can better reflect our values				
Leading Change				
7. We expect to have a positive influence on the process of change				
8. We appreciate the need for change and have energy and enthusiasm for making things better				
9. We have a compelling purpose that influences and informs the changes we make				

Innovation

	4	3	2	1

10. We are encouraged and enabled to innovate

11. We are able to learn from trial and error in the process of innovation

12. We innovate in order to fulfil our core purpose more effectively

Motivation

13. Our diverse intrinsic motivators are recognised and nurtured

14. We are highly motivated, work to our strengths and as a result find our work fulfilling

15. We understand and share our core purpose; there are high levels of motivation here

Engagement

16. We are encouraged to work to our strengths and find fulfilment in our work

17. There is a commitment to ensuring that we thrive and become fully immersed in our work

18. We have a clarity of purpose that inspires us and results in total engagement

SECTION B

This section is about how individual people feel and their experience of working in the organisation.
Please score the following descriptors.
4= true 3=mostly true 2=partially true 1=not true

Alignment	4	3	2	1
1. I feel responsible for the success of the organisation and know my work matters				
2. I feel we all agree about what is important				
3. I believe in what we are trying to do				
4. I am committed to high standards				
5. I am clear about our aims and know what is most important				
Climate Creation				
6. I experience a generosity of spirit in the way we help and support each other				
7. I feel physically and psychologically safe at work				
8. I experience a high degree of harmony with my colleagues				
9. I am able to resolve differences through open discussion				
10. I know that unprofessionalism will be challenged effectively				

Diagnostic Checklist: Improving from WithIn

Leading Change	4	3	2	1

11. I know that the ideas I have about what needs to change are valued and help shape the future

12. I am able to make changes to improve the way I work

13. I can freely express my ideas and opinions about changes that take place here

14. I have opportunities to influence how change is implemented

15. I see the need for change and enjoy making things better

Innovation				

16. I discover new ways of working by experimenting

17. I am able to learn from mistakes and try something else

18. I experience a high degree of creativity in the way we work

19. I talk with my colleagues as we endeavour to find new ways to do things

20. When I have new ideas, I am excited about testing them out at work

Motivation				

21. I get a sense of achievement from my work

22. I look forward to coming to work

23. I enjoy learning and discovering ways to improve my work

24. I meet the challenges at work with enthusiasm

25. I am aware of my strengths and use these in my work

Engagement	4	3	2	1
26. I can decide how to do my work and as a result feel able to perform at my best				
27. I often get absorbed in my work				
28. I love the work I do and am happy to 'go the extra mile' to make things better				
29. I enjoy reflecting on my work and often think of ways to improve				
30. I thrive at work				

INTERPRETING THE RESULTS

General

When using diagnostic tools and questionnaires, it is helpful to look for variations in response: for example, the person who scores everything at a 3 and then for one section or question scores very differently. When multiple respondents score a particular section or question in a similar way, that is a trend and your focus is drawn to it. However, when working with questionnaire results, it is the variation that tells you the most.

I would be curious if one of the dimensions scored significantly higher than others. That would indicate that that dimension is well established within the organisation. If one is lower, that's where further investigation would be helpful to identify exactly what the reasons are behind this.

My own preference in using such tools is a mix of questionnaires that are anonymised, and group or individual conversations to discover the reasons for the results.

Specific Nuance in Questions

Section A

Questions 1, 4, 7, 10, 13 and 16 focus on autonomy.
Questions 2, 5, 8, 11, 14 and 17 focus on mastery.
Questions 3, 6, 9, 12, 15 and 18 focus on purpose.

APPENDIX

MCKINSEY 7-S-BASED DIAGNOSTIC TOOL

The following are diagnostic questions that can be used to help understand the complexity of organisations and where to focus priorities for change. Originally designed by the 3D team at HTI for use in schools, the questions are equally applicable for other sectors. We've adapted the language to suit our context and concepts that were familiar to the teams we worked with.

To use the statements in your organisation, create a questionnaire and ask respondents to score, on a 6 or 10-point scale, how true they are.

I include here the link to a full explanation of the model from McKinsey:

www.mckinsey.com/business-functions/strategy-and-corporate-finance/our-insights/enduring-ideas-the-7-s-framework

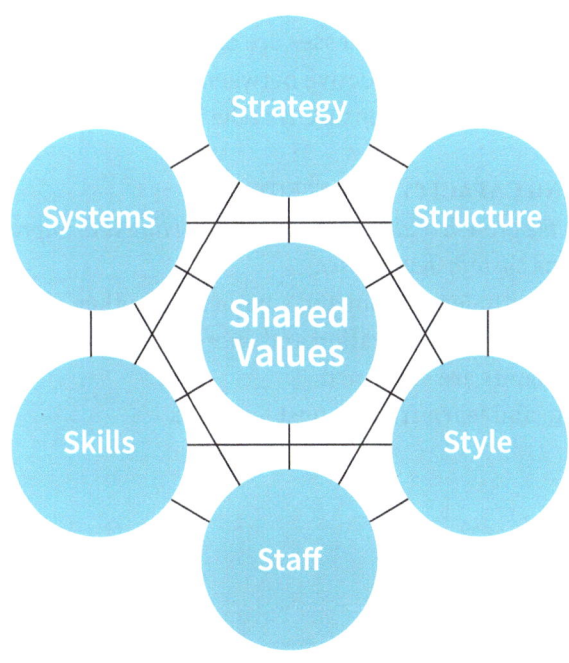

VISION (SHARED VALUES)
Is about the way we create a vision of our preferred future and how we communicate this in order to realise it.
Every adult can articulate the vision accurately
The vision is shared by all
Everyone is committed to realising the vision
Everyone knows the key actions they need to take to realise it

ORGANISATION (STRUCTURE)
Is about establishing the way things are structured in order to deliver the vision. It is about clarity of roles, responsibilities and lines of accountability.
The way we are organised is fit for purpose
Lines of accountability are used effectively
All staff are clear about their roles and responsibilities
The structure enables us to achieve our goals

SYSTEMS
Is about the way we create effective mechanisms in order to get things done. It implies effective communication, transparent and clear decision-making, and implementation of actions.
Our systems enable us to do what we need to do
Our decision-making processes are clear and transparent
Communications are effective between people at all levels
Systems are in place to ensure that decisions are implemented

BUILDING CAPACITY (STRATEGY)
Is about the growth of the organisation, enabling it to improve from within and sustain development.
We share with, learn from and support each other
There is sufficient motivation and energy to implement change
Improvements are sustained
We invite and learn from honest feedback

CLIMATE (STYLE)
Is about creating the right conditions in which people can work effectively in order to achieve shared goals.
There is a positive climate which enables all staff to give their best
The organisation is brave enough to deal with unprofessional behaviours
We resolve our differences and conflicts with integrity
There is agreement on a common set of values

LEADERSHIP (SKILLS, INSTITUTIONAL AND INDIVIDUAL)
Is about the behaviours and qualities of the people who drive the vision. Successful leaders influence others using a range of styles and skills.
Leaders at all levels are self-aware and manage themselves and others effectively
All leaders use an appropriate leadership style for each situation
There is a commitment to developing leadership and management skills
Staff at all levels accept that they have leadership responsibilities

HUMAN RESOURCES (STAFF)
Is about ensuring that all staff have the capacity, competence and commitment to fulfil their role.
Staff have the appropriate skills, attitudes and knowledge to do their job
Professional development is focused on organisational goals and objectives
Staff can innovate and create change
Staff are highly motivated and demonstrate their commitment to goals and objectives

Thanks and Acknowledgements

I want to thank the people who have contributed to this work, either by encouraging me and cheering me on or by more specific inputs. Firstly, for the warmth of response from Waverley Abbey Trust in accepting this work for publication and Joy McIlroy who has held my hand through the publishing process. I was at Waverley Abbey in 2019 at a retreat and met Bob Stradling from Waverley Abbey College over a coffee. Our conversations planted the seed for this book and I was always convinced that its home would be Waverley. Bob and I discussed the material as the focus for a PhD or research MA but something in me resisted this and I am grateful to Dave Trotman from Newman University who met with me during this time and concluded, 'Sue you don't need to do further study, you know what you want to say and have already researched, just write it'.

During the writing process I was accompanied by Rev Derek Holbird who I had met as a colleague at Church of England education events. Derek kindly read early versions of the manuscript and offered his thoughts. One critical suggestion he made was, 'I would be interested to find out what other Christian Leaders thought about this', and chapter 10 was born as a result. The interviews I conducted with those 15 Christian leaders, all over Zoom and during lockdown, were the richest of conversations, full of wisdom. I hope I have done justice to them in my writing. The book would not have been as deep without them. I want to thank them, unnamed to preserve anonymity, they know who they are.

In writing the first two chapters I revisited much of my career journey and became aware of the many people who had influenced or championed me and my work. Some gave me opportunities and opened doors to finding the golden threads I have written about. My particular thanks to Professor Sir Tim Brighouse who demonstrated qualities of leadership that have become legendary in the education sphere. Tim invested in me, and I got to see his kindness, wisdom, and humility close up. Recently I met him at an event and his warmth and encouragement continues to this day. He asked if I would send him my book to read which was affirming as always.

The opening of the National College for School Leadership in 2000 was a government initiative that shaped a generation of school leaders, for me personally it gave opportunities to grow, learn and contribute to the development of thought leadership in education. Most significant of all it gave me access to ideas, research and affirmed me in my thinking. As a Lead Facilitator and Subject Specialist, gained a community of practice and developed valued friendships. Some of those colleagues also became 'team' as we worked through HTI to deliver programmes in the West Midlands. Of those I want to thank Tony Graham who was the first colleague I shared the model Improving from WithIn with. I remember him debating the model, questioning the rationale, and interrogating my thinking. He then encouraged me to share it with others and we began to work together on the diagnostic questionnaire which is included at the end of the text. Tony's intellectual curiosity, encouragement and generosity of time was invaluable to the early development of the model.

During my association with HTI, Anita Wheeler set up the 3D team; the camaraderie, depth of thinking and generosity of the core team was an experience I will always cherish. Anita has become a precious friend and we got to work together again when she was Director of Teach First West Midlands and I was in my role at Coventry Diocese, since then, just for fun we have continued to create programmes and deliver training together.

I want to thank the many school leaders and teachers who have allowed me into their schools and classrooms. As I worked with you, I developed a respect for the profession that still drives me to champion you. I believe you are incredible in your ability to show up each day and face the challenges of the classroom, delivering imaginative and engaging teaching. Your resourcefulness and sacrificial communication which each day requires you to share yourselves is vastly under-recognised. I long for a day when you are valued and given the professional confidence to conduct your craft aligned to your educational philosophy.

Away from the education world I have had the privilege to work with church and third sector leaders, I am grateful for their trust as I have been able to flex across existing sector boundaries. My learning that much of the experience of leaders is similar across sectors and the solutions to the challenges are found in the same wisdom.

I owe a huge debt to Riverside Church in Birmingham who had faith in my leadership and entrusted me with the roles of trustee and then Chair of Trustees over many years. Riverside has been my home and family since 1988 and formative in the lives of my husband and children. As chair, I experienced the complexity of balancing faith and the demands of the charity commission, leading change from within an organisation whilst navigating difficult conversations and decisions which had implications for those I cared deeply about.

I had no comprehension of how long the process of getting this work into print would take and of how valuable the input of those willing to read and comment on early versions of the manuscript would be. I want to thank my early readers, Val Eagan, Paul Duncan, Helen Farquharson, Judy Moore, Andy Worthington, Alison Cansdale, and Neil Flint, their willingness to engage with my work and to give me feedback has been the encouragement I have needed to face the vulnerability of sharing my work more widely.

In the coaching profession, the work of Professor Peter Hawkins is widely respected, he generously gave me his time to discuss my work, he challenged my thinking, made some suggestions and most helpful of all, gave me the confidence to commit to the Christian distinctiveness of my work.

REFERENCES

1. www.youtube.com/watch?v=MwG3MLJkWT0
2. Sue Iqbal, Andrew Cooper, *Benchmarks for School Ethos* (Birmingham: Birmingham Health Education Unit, 2001)
3. Daniel H. Pink, *Drive* (New York: Riverhead Books, 2009); www.danpink.com/books/drive/
4. www.youtube.com/watch?v=iG9CE55wbtY
5. www.mckinsey.com/business-functions/strategy-and-corporate-finance/our-insights/enduring-ideas-the-7-s-framework
6. Estelle Morris, 'Teaching Needs Less Ideology, and More Evidence', *The Guardian*, 25 November 2014
7. www.cambridgeindependent.co.uk/education/cambridge-academic-says-target-driven-culture-is-leading-to-increase-in-depression-among-health-workers-9053769/
8. https://assets.publishing.service.gov.uk/government/uploads/system/uploads/attachment_data/file/457392/Common_20Inspection_20Framework_20for_20further_20education_20and_20skills_20from_20September_202012.pdf
9. www.wholeeducation.org/
10. www.nfer.ac.uk/flipped-learning-research-report
11. Richard Boyatzis, 'An Overview of Intentional Change from a Complexity Perspective', *Journal of Management Development*, 8 January 2006
12. Edward T. Hall, Iceberg Model of Culture, 1976
13. Boyatzis, 2004
14. Sue Iqbal, Values for Learning Project, 1996
15. Tom Peters and Robert H. Waterman Jr, *In Search of Excellence* (New York: Harper Collins, 1982)
16. Christopher M. Branson, 'Achieving Organisational Change Through Values Alignment', *Journal of Educational Administration*, Volume 46, No 3, 2007, page 376
17. www.coventrycathedral.org.uk/
18. Richard E Boyatzis, 2000
19. 'Intentional Change Theory at an Organizational Level', Van Oesten, *Journal of Management Development*, Volume 25, Issue 7
20. Everett M. Rogers, *Diffusion of Innovations*, 5th Edition (New York: Free Press, 2003)
21. McClelland Center of Research and Innovation, Boston, MA. Presented in Hay Group Managerial Style Workbook through Korn Ferry Leadership Style Workbook
22. Sir John Whitmore, *Coaching for Performance: The Principles and Practices of Coaching and Leadership* (Boston: Nicholas Brealey Publishing, 1992)
23. Patrick Lencioni, *The Advantage*, 1st Edition (New York: Jossey-Bass, 2012)
24. Matt Bawden, https://sec-ed.co.uk/best-practice-school-ethos-vision-and-aspiration
25. Samuel R. Chand, *Cracking Your Church's Culture Code: Seven Keys to Unleashing Vision and Inspiration* (San Francisco: Jossey-Bass, 2010)
26. Will Mancini, *Church Unique: How Missional Leaders Cast Vision, Capture Culture, and Create Movement* (San Francisco: Jossey-Bass, 2008)
27. GRPI model 1972 in Richard Beckhard, 'Optimizing team-building efforts', Journal of Contemporary Business 1.3, Seattle, 1972, pp.23–32
28. Sue Iqbal, May 2020
29. SWOT Analysis en.wikipedia.org/wiki/SWOT_analysis
30. Kubler-Ross Change Curve, www.ekrfoundation.org/5-stages-of-grief/change-curve/
31. Permission to use granted by John Fisher July 2021
32. Sue Iqbal, 2020
33. Leadership That Gets Results, Daniel Goleman, Harvard Business Review March/April 2000
34. 'Johari Window', Joseph Luft and Harrington Ingham, 1955
35. Leadership Style Workbook available from www.store.kornferry.com

36 www.spaceforgrace.network
37 https://www.dur.ac.uk/creativitycommission/report/recommendations/
38 https://theconversation.com/creativity-is-a-human-quality-that-exists-in-every-single-one-of-us-92053
39 Gardner, H. (1983). *Frames of Mind: A Theory of Multiple Intelligences*. New York: Basic Books
40 https://pastors.com/?s=innovation+in+church 6 Ways to Create a Culture of Innovation in Your Church Rick Warren, 17th June 2017
41 Maslow, Abraham H. (1943). "A theory of human motivation". *Psychological Review* Vol. 50 (4): 370–396.
42 David McClelland, *The Achieving Society* (Cambridge: Cambridge University Press, 1961)
43 Daniel H. Pink, *Drive: The Surprising Truth About What Motivates Us*, (New York: Riverhead Books, 2009)
44 Edward L. Deci and Richard Ryan, *Intrinsic Motivation and Self-Determination in Human Behavior* (Boston MA: Springer, 1985)
45 Daniel H. Pink, *Drive: The Surprising Truth About What Motivates Us*, (New York: Riverhead Books, 2009), page 72
46 Mihaly Csikszentmihalyi, *Finding Flow: The Psychology of Engagement with Everyday Life* (New York: Basic Books, 1998)
47 Daniel H. Pink, *Drive: The Surprising Truth About What Motivates Us*, (New York: Riverhead Books, 2009), page 90
48 Carol Dweck, *Mindset* (London: Little Brown Book Group, 2012)
49 Daniel H. Pink, *Drive: The Surprising Truth About What Motivates Us*, (New York: Riverhead Books, 2009), page 125
50 Daniel H. Pink, *Drive: The Surprising Truth About What Motivates Us*, (New York: Riverhead Books, 2009), page 133
51 Daniel H. Pink, *Drive: The Surprising Truth About What Motivates Us*, (New York: Riverhead Books, 2009), page 134
52 www.bridgepastoral.org.uk/history/frankLake.htm
www.bridgepastoral.org.uk/dynamic-cycle.htm
53 April 1991
54 Martin Seligman, *The Journal of Positive Psychology* 16 February 2018, Volume 13 Issue 4 pages 333-335
55 www.PositivePsychology.com
56 https://eprints.kingston.ac.uk/id/eprint/4192/1/19wempen.pdf, series 19, October 2008
57 William A. Kahn, https://eprints.kingston.ac.uk/id/eprint/4192/1/19wempen.pdf, series 19, October 2008 *Academy of Management Journal*, Volume 33, No. 4, 1990, page 3
58 https://eprints.kingston.ac.uk/id/eprint/4192/1/19wempen.pdf
59 John Storey, *Leadership in Organizations, 3rd edition* (London: Routledge, 2016)
60 Engaging for Success: enhancing performance through employee engagement. A report to Government by David MacLeod and Nita Clarke (2009 Crown Copyright)
61 Mihaly Csikszentmihalyi, *Finding Flow: The Psychology of Engagement with Everyday Life* (New York: Basic Books, 1998)
62 Mihaly Csikszentmihalyi, *Flow: The Psychology of Optimal Experience* (New York: Harper and Row, 1990), page 3
63 www.myersbriggs.org/my-mbti-personality-type/mbti-basics
64 Further information available from www.enneagramacademy.com/enneagram-test/
65 www.careynieuwhof.com/5-reasons-why-engagement-is-the-new-church-attendance/
66 Sue Iqbal, Signposts Coaching, 2008
67 Zunin and Myers, the model Phases of Collective Trauma (1990), cited in D. J. DeWolfe, Training Manual for Mental Health and Human Service Workers in Major Disasters (US Department of Human Services), Section 2, page 5

WAVERLEY ABBEY COLLEGE

Develop your gifts • Be equipped • Make a difference

Equipping people to be the positive impact on society through courses in:

- Counselling
- Spiritual Formation
- Contemporary courses in Chaplaincy, Discipleship and Church Ministry

waverleyabbeycollege.ac.uk

Spiritual Formation

See your faith and life transformed, and be equipped and empowered to make a Christ-like difference in society

Undergraduate

BA (Hons) Top-Up in Spiritual Formation

This programme is suitable for those interested in spiritual formation both for themselves and in helping others that they interact with to grow and develop spiritually.

Postgraduate

Postgraduate Certificate in Spiritual Direction

This programme is suitable for those interested in becoming or developing themselves in an existing role as a Spiritual Director.

waverleyabbeycollege.ac.uk